A Minor Poet In A Minor Key

Michael Incitti

DEDICATION

This book is dedicated to my wife, Aprile, and to my children, Marc, Marissa and Chelsea. But it is primarily dedicated to my daughter, Marissa, who by learning the publishing business made this work possible.

"The most beautiful thing we can experience is the mysterious. It is the source of all true art and science." – Albert Einstein

TABLE OF CONTENTS

Chapter 3 One Child Saved   65

Chapter 4 All My Tomorrows   95

FOREWORD

I never knew my father had a secret life as a poet and a lyricist. It is his passion and his craft, and he has pursued it with an almost obsessive-compulsive drive for decades. For the most part, he always seemed composed and outwardly calm. Inside though, I know now that his mind was going a mile a minute, taking in impressions and ideas and running them through the mill of his imagination. I never knew my father was also an incorrigible night owl. I always thought he was downstairs watching the sports channel or a science fiction movie. Instead he was in our basement seated at his piano working on the only dream he ever had and that he has carried with him nearly all of his life – songwriting. That he could command and discipline these traits to produce lyric poetry and musical compositions from his imagination is a testament to his determination and to his indomitable will. But time and circumstance compelled him to work at other things in order to make a living and to provide for his family.

Before my sister and I and my brother were born, he worked in journalism as a newspaper reporter and a sportswriter. By the time my brother was born Dad had a scholarship to graduate school. He taught journalism and media law at the college level for over a decade. But instead of migrating Mom and us kids across the country in search of an elusive tenure, he used his natural business instincts and practical nature to forge a career in finance as an investment adviser. He did this so that our family could remain in one place as we grew up. When my brother and sister and I were children he always found time to play sports with us, and in fact to coach some of our teams in baseball and basketball. Athletics was the classroom he used to teach us about life. As of this writing he's still involved in scholastic sports as a basketball and soccer referee, and a baseball umpire.

But I think his greatest teachings come from his writing, from the poems and lyrics contained in this book. He talks about life and love to such an extent that the depth of his soul comes through on every page. This work is by no means comprehensive. My father selected the poems and lyrics he thought were most representative of his ability, and that presented a balanced array of thematic explorations over a variety of time periods. He also chose the ones he liked best and that often had an interesting story surrounding their creation.

That was my idea, to include aspects of his creative process. Part of my motivation was to learn how he did it. But I still don't know. He never studied music formally, although he sang in choirs and as a soloist. He is self-taught vocally and on piano. As for the poems and lyrics he writes, even he is at a loss to say where they come from. He says "Sometimes you just know. It can begin with a word or a phrase, and I'll know right away I can build it into a tangible piece that tells a story."

As my brother and sister and I got older, he would occasionally ask us our opinion. "Hey, how does this sound?" And he'd play a few bars of music. Or he'd recite a few lines of his poetry and say "Does it sound better like this, or like this?" We'd give him our opinion and he'd invariably laugh. With a crooked grin and a twinkle in his eyes he'd head back to his piano, like the "wild-man wizard" in a song by Harry Chapin, one of his favorites. Dad learned by studying the masters. He said that's the best way to learn how to write and to make music. Then you go do it. He said whatever you write has to come from your soul. If you listen closely enough, you'll hear my father's soul in every line of every page.

Marissa Incitti

Three Black Cats Publishing

April 2016

INTRODUCTION

Communications technology has advanced at the speed of light, but I still rely on the traditional story-telling methods of the journalist's eye and the poet's voice. With a pen and a yellow legal pad always near, I have sought to capture those elements that inspire examination and celebration from novelists, essayists, poets and songwriters. One of my core traits as a writer is the ability to uncover the motivation of a subject, why a person does what he or she does. This is in keeping with the literary tradition that character informs plot. I am also blessed, or cursed, with a powerful memory that allows me to recall dialogue, setting and mood over decades. These abilities help me realize my vision of telling simple stories in a clear and plain voice. Coupled with my love of music, the drive to write songs and poetry has accompanied me all of my life.

This book has the dual purpose of representing my first published collection of poetry and lyrics, as well as being a capstone project toward a graduate degree in publishing for my daughter, Marissa. So, as her father, my first responsibility was to make certain that the work helped her graduate. My daughter was instrumental in having commentary attached to many of the poems herein. She felt that to include discussion of how and when the work came about, the inspirations for the end result or the circumstances that surrounded it, would further distinguish it from other books of poetry. It might also shed light on the creative process within a literary framework. Most poets and songwriters, most artists generally, leave those elements to mystery, thus creating not only a mystique for their work, but a context for readership that allows for multiple interpretations. We believe the attendant commentary may enhance the reader's enjoyment and engagement, but also leave room for the reader to attach meaning.

Artistic pursuit is distinguished from flights of fancy by the deliberate and measured investigation of a subject, almost to the point of obsession. And nothing short of completing it will be acceptable, whether it takes 30 minutes, or 30 years. It is sometimes cathartic in overall effect. But the mere act of creating these works was overwhelmingly satisfying. When words fell into place or phrases matched an established rhythm and meter – when I got it to say what I wanted it to say – I felt blessed.

Where these works came from other than my imagination is still a mystery. At times I would assign a work to myself because I liked a topic or an idea. But the lion's share of the time the inspiration came out of thin air, most often when I was doing something else entirely. It would appear as a phrase or a fragment of a line that had that ping to it, and then it was up to me to sculpt the rest of the work from my imagination and build it into something tangible and complete. All I know is these works had to be written, regardless of the time of day.

As a rule, ideas would come late at night when all was quiet, or very early in the morning. They might begin with a spoken word or a phrase. Other times a complete 4-line stanza would repeat in my mind and drive me to the table to write. Then like a cloudburst the work would pour out over the page. I was often left with a sense of gratification that something had been given to me, and my role was as an intermediary or a vessel simply to give it form. As this work is a reflection of my inner-visions and meditations through a poetic and literary looking glass, it is essentially the story of a life. But its primary purpose is to give life to the works herein.

What a happy confluence of events that one of my children would enjoy books and reading to such an extent that she would undertake graduate study in book publishing after starting out in journalism. My daughter, Marissa, had no idea that I had a manuscript waiting, a book without an identity. So for the opportunity to collaborate with my ambitious and diplomatic daughter, Marissa, on a project that has occupied a central part of my life for decades, and that will help her in her career, well, it leaves me nearly beyond words. And for a wordsmith that's a rare state of being. So this journey has been nothing less than amazing, filled with surprise and delight at pushing the boundaries of my imagination. I had been too driven to create the work to ever find time to publish it or market it to any extent. That my daughter will take up that mantle is almost poetic in itself.

In my time I have been many things. But my greatest role has always been as a family man: the husband of my beautiful wife, and the father of my three blessed children. In between all that these roles demanded, I kept my dream alive to be a songwriter. This work is a testament to that noble goal.

Of the 101 lyric poems in this volume presented in 99 entries, I have written music to 24 of them. For me, melody comes more slowly than lyrics. I have been a singer – tenor/baritone - for most of my adult life, and I play self-taught piano enough to designate a key signature and hammer out a tune with a melody line and accompanying chords. It is a solitary process that I embrace, but it must be cultivated and driven.

The inspirations for works of note have been discussed in literary circles for centuries. The present volume is not a work of note – yet. But I've long believed that when ideas come they are gifts from God, and as such they demand to be written to the best of one's ability. To ignore that spark would be to fall short of one's responsibility to fulfill a calling. Writing then is my spiritual food, like a child eating bread and milk. That's me on the book cover at age 2 with a PBJ and a cup of milk in my "office" -- the back porch of my childhood home.

"Daily Bread" almost became the title of this book. But my daughter, the publisher, didn't like it, or its religious overtones. I said to her, well then, we'll title it by what it is. So, "A Minor Poet In A Minor Key" came to be. The title's humility comes through because of my great respect and admiration for the artists mentioned in this book. A touch of lyricism is also present because like all of my work, it speaks the truth. Dear reader, enjoy.

Michael A. Incitti

November 2015

CHAPTER 1
SUM OF ITS PARTS

REVERIE

Do my eyes deceive me?
Was something there in yours?
Something meant for me alone,
A key to unlock your door.

How can I convince you,
Uncertain and unappeased?
A pawn of clay in a lover's game,
Where you hold the expertise.

The beauty you share just standing there
Makes me move with tender haste.
Your hair of gold, your eyes of blue,
The curve of your slender waist.

I long to hold you close,
To touch your hair, your face.
You paint an indelible picture,
A portrait of style and grace.

Only time will tell us
What my heart believes is true.
You were meant for me, my love,
And I was meant for you.

I want you to love me
For more than this moment in time.
To have and to hold, a girl of my own,
Until poets run out of rhyme.

Bridge

I see us together on distant shores
Walking by the sea.
Hand in hand, waves in the sand,
Rushing over our feet.

I hold you close and we embrace
Sunlight streaming all around.
Seagulls cry in the clouds above,
But we don't hear a sound.
Now I stand before you,
An unspoken love to proclaim.
I reach for you and then I see
Your heart is not the same.

Your eyes just looked beyond me
To another that you adore.
It's sad to see, but it's not me.
You turned and closed your door.

Then I remembered
What a wise man said
A long, long time ago.
That fools rush in,
My only sin,
Where angels fear to go.
Because fools rush in,
My only sin,
Where angels fear to go.

NOTES: This was a song that wouldn't let me sleep. It was written in two bursts from 3 to 4 a.m. and 5:45 to 6:30 a.m. in late December 2006. The first stanza came then the rest followed. But this work required editing and polishing. The original title was "Fools Rush In," but that sounded familiar and I discovered it was a Frank Sinatra song with lyrics by the great Johnny Mercer. So "Reverie" stood. This song represented an awakening of the creative process in me that had long been dormant – material that compelled action to create, words and rhythms overlaid with images and dreams that had to be recorded. Over the next 9 years my creative output would hit a peak presenting a distillation of my accumulated literary abilities. The works that followed through the years were really nothing more than faithful and true recordings of what was in my mind's eye rendered by the artistic and literary voice that God gave me.

THE LOVER AND THE BELOVED

1st Verse:

The sun pours through the window
And its light divides the room.
You sit in the shadows with secrets,
The kind my questions can't consume.

Something's different your hair, your face,
Your lips, your eyes of blue.
We are torn by what we want,
And by what we have to do.

Chorus:

In every romance there is the lover and the beloved.
We cannot escape nature's ways.
We throw caution to the wind with a vow we can't rescind
To find someone with whom to spend our days.

2nd Verse:

The vision of her lingers
Like a shadow on the wall,
Her silhouette dances
As evening starts to fall.

She comes to me in a ruby red robe,
With only herself underneath.
I kiss her lightly on the lips
And unwrap the present she bequeaths.

Chorus:

In every romance there is the lover and the beloved.
We cannot escape nature's ways.
We throw caution to the wind with a vow we can't rescind
To find someone with whom to spend our days.

Bridge:

Baseball teams in America
Play one-hundred and sixty-two games.
As September wanes
Fans sit on needles and pins.
Across the Atlantic in Great Britain,
They got millions of people live by the Thames.
Very precise and sometimes twice as nice,
But they don't give a damn who wins.

3rd Verse:

The heart has its reasons
That reason never knows.
The eyes tell the story
To the depths of the soul.

The lover and the beloved
Is a dance time can't transcend.
It's a game with a beginning and a middle,
But it never comes to an end.

Chorus:

In every romance there is a lover and a beloved.
We cannot escape nature's ways.
We throw caution to the wind with a vow we can't rescind
To find someone with whom to spend our days.

NOTES: This song came to me as I thought about the concept of the lover and the beloved as an observable relationship phenomenon, often explored in literature. If you read closely you might see some influence from one of my favorite composers and poets, Paul Simon. He covers similar themes, and his use of imagery and mood are among the most literary and brilliant of all popular musicians.

I'M NOT THE ONE

Girl, you want me to help you run your life,
When I have a life of my own.
Why is it we can't meet in the middle?
Why is my time always on loan?

You make the dates, you make the appointments.
I make the money, and take all the blame.
You make the scene, you won't get a replacement.
I buy the tickets and forget my own name.

Something gets lost in translation
Whenever our two worlds collide.
Sometimes my face is in your rear-view mirror --
I'm just along for the ride.

Chorus:

I'm not the one who will tell all your secrets,
I'm not the one who'll sell all your lies.
I'm not the one who your friends need to speak with.
I'm not the one who will hand you alibis.

I'm not the one who will run in your sweet dream.
I'm not the one who will help you stay sane.
I'm not the one who's the coffee to your cream.
I'm not the one who will wait in the rain.

The virtuous reward themselves
With an uncertain sense of grace.
They whisper their love, and assert their hate
While falling behind in the race.

You keep your hidden persona
Wrapped up in satin and lace.
The veil that shrouds your motives
Is drawn by the lines on your face.

We spend our days in longing
For that which we cannot reach.
Is it wrong to want things beyond our grasp,
With a drive you just can't impeach?

Chorus:

Bridge:

Your romance escapes me,
I know you don't hate me,
But this feeling keeps bringing me down.
I know that you care for me,
You say you'll be there for me,
But tell me why you're not around?

Something gets lost in translation
Whenever our two worlds collide.
Sometimes my face is in your rear-view mirror --
I'm just along for the ride.

Chorus:

Repeat and fade

NOTES: This work arose from a growing confidence with written words and the freedom to experiment with their limitless possibilities. I began with the chorus. The bridge followed soon after, both driven heavily by rhythm and cadence. The chorus and bridge came to me in a burst while working outside in early summer. I remember responding to an inquiry from my wife about who put what where, and I said quite plainly, "Well, I'm not the one." Once I knew what the song was about, the rest followed quickly.

PRESENT TENSE WOMAN

1st Verse:

1st Verse:

She lives in the moment,
Her future isn't planned.
Her past is gone
Like a fist full of sand.

The more you try to hold her
The faster she runs away.
With eyes that spark and smolder,
One glance and you'll obey.

She's a planet in your galaxy
Moving fast without a moon.
Her orbit has no gravity.
She will make you dance and swoon.

She's really very pretty,
And you know she's got some cash.
She likes high heels late at night,
And she'll help you with your rash.

Chorus:

She's a present tense woman,
Right now is all she knows.
She's a present tense woman
Who casts her own kind of glow.

She's a present tense woman,
She'll beat you at your game.
She's a present tense woman,
The kind you'll never tame.

Bridge:

Impetuous yes
But you chose to acquiesce
And give in to your ardent desires.
If she had to guess

She would say you are a mess,
But she still wants to take you that much higher.
You spoke of your unease
And she knows you tried to please
When what you did was almost spousal.
But you didn't realize
That your senses were alive
And firing at the peak of your arousal.
She makes no pretense
With no advice to dispense.
But your life she will condense until you see.

Chorus:

2nd Verse:

She will bring you to your knees
In no time at all.
You will long to be free
Of her haunting siren call.

When she walks down the street
A million eyes follow.
She leads her own parade
And she'll leave you feeling hollow.

No one would accuse her --
She's not that type of girl.
You might want to use her,
Might like to take a whirl.

But she will only chastise you
And kick you out the door.
She'll laugh at your audacity
Like a hundred times before.

Chorus, repeat and fade

© 2010, Michael A. Incitti

NOTES: This was a work of pure imagination. The title character could be any woman who held a man entranced or spellbound.

THE EAGLE AND THE DOVE

Intro.

I see the devil in the field where the bodies lay,
He laughed at God because he had his way.
There's no turning back now, the blood was spilled.
And the devil drank his fill.

1st Verse:

I stood shoulder to shoulder in the middle of the crowd.
Turned away wondering what will happen to us now.
The men with the answers have all gone away --
Taken before we had a chance to pray.

If history is our destiny then our fate's already been written.
We can't change the past, but there are lessons if we listen.
The complexities of the world sometimes compel our action.
Even the least of us knows we are weakened by subtraction.

Chorus:

The voices of Dixie, Vietnam and Iraq
Cry out in vain to halt the attack.
High on a hill a bell rings through the rain.
On a dark November day
The torch was passed
To find a peace that lasts.

Bridge:

Three half-centuries have come and gone.
Lincoln's words echo through troubadour's souls.
When will we learn to honor his wisdom?
Instead we fight for a useless control,
Toward an undefined goal,
As the devil calls the roll,
And war takes its toll.

Bridge continued:

Grant and McClelland, Jackson and Lee,
Patton, MacArthur, and Westmoreland could see
No one wants to die because their country has decreed.
Freedom, independence, and liberty too,
Get tangled with the sins of the elected few.

Chorus:

The voices of Dixie, Vietnam and Iraq,
Cry out in vain to halt the attack.
High on a hill a bell rings through the rain.
On a dark November day
The torch was passed
To find a peace at last.

2nd Verse:

But now we all find there's no compromise.
The men in the suits keep putting down lies.
There's no restitution for the multitude who died,
Except to say they tried.

And what of the lost who will never come home?
Will we honor their memory with scattered ashes over foam?
Or will we spread the word of freedom and not drive it with war.
Are we asking too much if peace is the cure?

Chorus:

2nd Bridge:

The truth lies with Dylan, and in the soaring voice of Joan.
They bring comfort to the wounded; the forgotten are not alone.
Baez and Bobby knocked down walls of hate,
Freed the prisoners of ideology, and told them it's not too late
To say we have no hand to lend
For a cause we won't defend
Fought by armies that refuse to bend,
While all around is war without end.

2nd Bridge continued:

Can the eagle fly on a path with the dove?
Can people try to replace hate with love?
Bobby and Joan we need you now,
To help put an end to the fighting somehow.

Chorus:

The voices of Dixie, Vietnam and Iraq,
Cry out in vain to halt the attack.
High on a hill a bell rings through the rain.
On a dark November day
The torch was passed
To find a peace at last.

NOTES: This is an anti-war song in the spirit of two powerful voices from the generation of the 1960s, singer-songwriters Bob Dylan and Joan Baez. A more indirect reference lies with one of my all-time favorite singer-songwriters, Billy Joel, "Goodnight, Saigon," and "Leningrad," as anti-war songs. But few songs capture the raw power of Joan Baez's "The Night They Drove Old Dixie Down," written by Robbie Robertson, or of Dylan's classic, "Blowin' In the Wind." In my song,' the dark November day' was the day Abraham Lincoln read his "Gettysburg Address," Nov. 19, 1863. The phrase "the torch was passed" is a reference to John F. Kennedy's inaugural address. Most other historical references are clear. While this ambitious and intentioned work covers a lot of historical ground, this is more of a written and spoken poem than one that is sung.

SUNDAY BEST

I save my Sunday best for you
With the innocence of a child.
I always want the rest of you
With a love so tender and mild.

If tomorrow takes me far away
I'll know today we loved.
My Sunday best is all I have,
Calm and peaceful as a dove.

There are things I want to tell you
That my heart won't let me say.
There are dreams I want to sell you,
But life keeps getting in the way.

Through it all we have each other,
No matter what life has in store.
Right from the start it's been just you and me,
Two hearts together at the core.

You know I can't always take you with me.
There are places where you cannot always go.
There are times when I don't understand what you do,
But I think there is something you should know.

I kept all the letters you wrote to me
When I went off to war.
Your words were my guardian angel.
It was you I was living for.

Whether we are near or far, my love,
Time stands still when you are gone.
Minutes pass like hours
Through the cold and lonely dawn.

But then I remember something you said
And it warms my heart like the rising sun.
I remember it from our earliest days –
Soon after I knew you were the one.

If love is true there's never too much,
There's only more love to give.
You make me blue by denying your touch.
I need your love to live.

I save my Sunday best for you
With the innocence of a child.
I always want the rest of you
With a love so tender and mild.
If tomorrow takes me far away
I'll know today we loved.
My Sunday best is all I have,
Calm and peaceful as a dove.

NOTES: I wrote this for my mother and my father, who were married at age 20 on July 3, 1941. Dad served in the U.S. Coast Guard during WWII from 1943 until the war ended in June 1945. They used to tell about how Mom drove, by herself, from Williamsport, Pa., to Virginia Beach, Va., in 1944, to meet Dad when he had shore leave at the Naval Base in Norfolk. It was a very long drive. My song in Chapter 7, "Summer Brunette," is another tribute to Mom and Dad, inspired by their shore leave. They were both born on a Sunday, hence the title. As children they lived through the Depression. They knew what it meant to do without. My father was always taciturn, so my goal with this song was to give voice to that which he could not express. I imagined these might have been Dad's words to Mom when he went off to war. The stanza that begins with "I kept all the letters you wrote to me," was a quote from Dad when recalling his time aboard ship in the Pacific. He said Mom's letters were his only companion. They stayed married for the next 68 years and 15 days until Mom passed in 2009. They never had much, but they always had each other. Like a classic car, maybe a 1953 Buick Roadmaster Skylark, white with a red interior and fat whitewall tires, they just don't make 'em like that anymore.

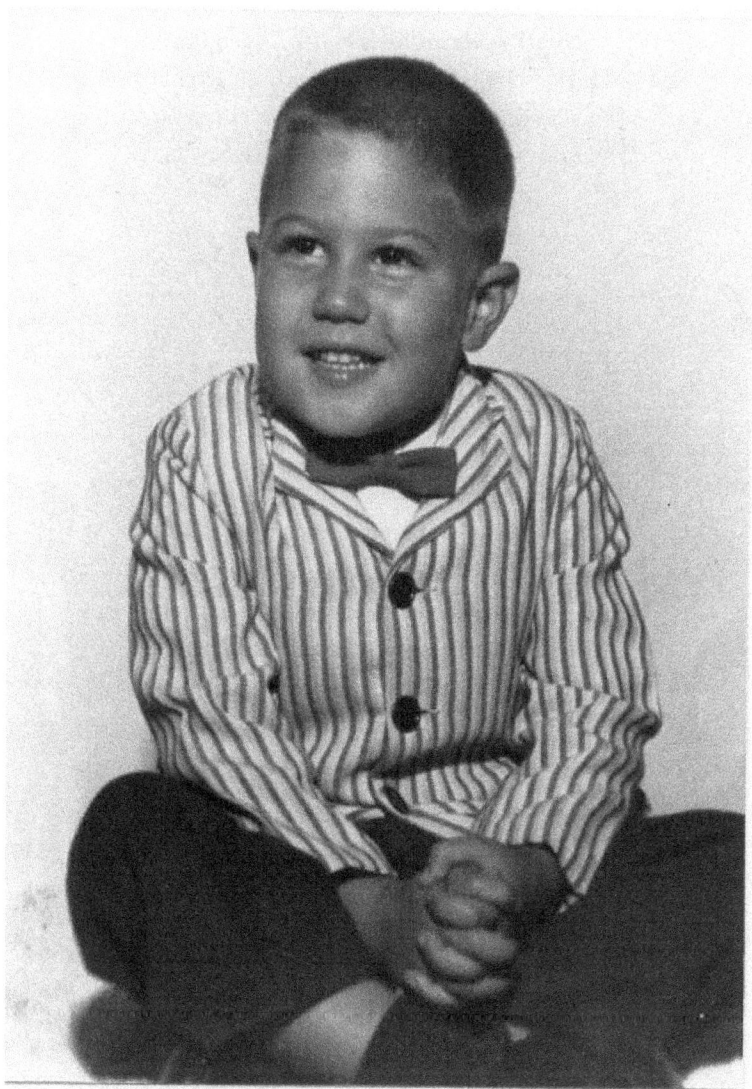

This is me at age 3 in my Sunday Best. My Mom took the photo.

CARRIED AWAY

The backyard cardinals lightly touch down,
Have a bite to eat, then they fly all around.
They remind us each day that we are as one.
Our lives together have only just begun.

There's something on my mind,
And I think you should know.
I'm crazy for you, girl,
And I'm gonna let it show.

But how can you say you love me
Without a passionate gaze?
How can you say you need me
Without leaving me in a daze?

I'm gonna take you everywhere,
Because I need you by my side.
Like the eagles that mate forever,
Our love will quietly abide.

The heart of a woman is an ocean deep,
With memories she discards and mementos
that she keeps.
But like the eagles in the sky we are carried away,
By a love sublime, to another time, another day.

© 2010, Michael A. Incitti

NOTES: This poem is stark in its simplicity. With cardinals and eagles --
birds that mate for life -- as a metaphor for a deep, abiding love between a
man and a woman, the poem achieves its purpose. I'm not a fan of odd-
numbered stanzas. I like them to bounce off each other. But you write what
the idea gives you and then you stop.

A BETTER WAY

1st Verse:

Takes the edge off,
Helps you cope
But don't you know
You ride a slippery slope?

All them little piggies
Just sittin' in a row,
Ain't got the sense
When it's time to go.

You tell me you want
To be emancipated,
And yet your reality
Is still negotiated.

Now I got no time
For crackheads like you.
It's time you went straight
Or your days are few.

So show me, don't tell me,
What you gonna do.
Time is gettin' late
'Fore your days are through.

You got no sense
Of time and space.
I hope you know
There's a much better place.

Chorus:

Crackhead
No, no, no, no, no, no, no, no
I said crackhead
Don't want no crackhead
Don't need no crackhead
No, no, no, no, no, no, no, no
I said crackhead

29

Chorus continued:

Don't want no crackhead
Don't need no crackhead
No, no, no, no, no, no, no, no
I said crackhead,
Gonna take you nowhere.
Crackhead,
Gonna git you dead.
Crackhead,
You won't go there.
Crackhead,
Listen to what I said.

2nd Verse:

You had nothin' to give
I said 'Make sure you receive
The message I bring
And just don't deceive.'

At first you didn't know
What you came here for,
But all I had for you
Was an open door.

Come on in
Let me give you a hand.
All you really need's
Someone to understand.

My little brother
Come from Michigan way.
I sure am proud
That he is here today.

Chorus:

3rd Verse:

I'm in Philly,
Taught at Simon Gratz.
Did my best each day
To keep out the rats.

I ain't talkin'
'Bout the ones that crawl.
I'm talkin' 'bout the ones
That write on the wall.

They tell you where to get
That very next high,
Meet 'em by the locker --
They'll sell you some lies.

I ran track
Twenty years ago.
Nine-six hundred --
Thought you should know.

Had some opportunity
Taken away
'Cause they said I used drugs,
But they made a mistake.

I ain't bitter
'Bout what I ain't got.
Now I work twice as hard
To improve my lot.

I take a lot of pride
In what I've done.
And now I help my brother
Learn a different type of fun.

He finally decided
To work a plan.
Now he's got the world
In the palm of his hand.

Found that he don't need
No dope to be
The kind of man
Our Momma always knew he could be.

I thank the Lord --
He helped us find a better way.
As God is my witness
This is our happy day.

Chorus:

4th Verse:

So you got no money
And you got no car.
But those ain't the things
That define who you are.

Who you are is someone
With the skill to achieve.
But if you don't use it
You might as well leave

Your hopes and your dreams
And your pride on the shelf
'Cause you need to believe
And rely on yourself.

In the streets
And the alleys too,
Schoolyard, classroom
I'm talkin' to you.

Crack ain't the way
To get where you want to be.
How many got to die
Before you'll see?

All my brothers and my sisters,
My message is clear.
The choice is yours,
The time is near.

Pay attention
To what I say.
Keep using crack --
In the ground you'll lay.

Chorus:

Repeat and fade

NOTES: This rap song came to me while I was cutting the grass at our home in Mountaintop, Pa., on May 21, 2007. One stanza after another kept flowing in my mind and it would not let me finish cutting the grass. I had to stop working, go in the house and write down each stanza as it came, then go back out and keep mowing the lawn. I don't know if the motion of pushing the lawn mower helped, but these words just kept coming and I wrote what I heard in my mind. There was no thematic, visual or musical antecedent. It just came to me and I wrote it. This process would be repeated many times over the next 9 years. It is representative of Wordsworth's definition of poetry, "The spontaneous overflow of powerful emotion." I wrote virtually all of this song while cutting the grass. I like its powerful message about redemption and fighting the war on drugs. It's a good message for junior high and high school kids, and they are my target audience. This was originally titled "Crackhead," but "A Better Way" is a more palatable and inviting title for a reader. Also, that's the result of what the characters found by rejecting drugs – a better way to live.

VACILLATION

She lingers over coffee
As the morning sun appears.
She wonders where the days have gone.
What's become of all the years?

What she thought would be
An interlude of joy
Was like trying to play
With a broken old toy.

Just when you think
You might make a decision,
Someone comes along
And says with precision

Exactly why you should not choose that direction.
Too bad cause you show a distinct predilection
Toward things that are fun and a pleasant diversion.
Find the center and complete your conversion.

Bridge:

But what did you give
To get what you got?
Is it something you just can't see?
When you look in the mirror
Is the answer getting clearer?
You know nothing comes for free.

Chorus:

Vacillation
Tell me what you see?
Vacillation
Can you tell that it's me?
Vacillation
Did you read all the signs?

34

Chorus continued:

Vacillation
These stars won't align.
Vacillation
Do you like me now?
Vacillation
Off the starboard bow?
Vacillation
Ain't no easy way.
Vacillation
Make your choice today.

2nd Verse:

I'm certain you are lovely,
Don't give that a second thought.
It's all about your state of mind
And what you do with what you've got.

I can never understand
What you are looking for.
Just take me by the hand,
Do I have to say more?

I see you in a trance of giddy expectation,
Waiting on a chance for which you never strive.
I see you in a dance of endless anticipation,
Planning for a future that never quite arrives.

Like a dance without a rhythm,
A song without a time,
A poem without meaning,
A mystery without a crime.

2nd Bridge:

I don't want to be an imposition
I don't want to launch an inquisition
But whatever happened to you and me?
In suspended animation
There's no room for proclamations,
But the answer is clear if you choose to see.

Chorus:

Minor Verse:

Time is an imposter
Stealing scenes from another life.
I cannot stop the larceny,
Can't mitigate the strife.

Ashes to ashes,
We all go down in flame.
Dust to dust,
Our fate is all the same.

Chorus:

Outro:

She lingers over coffee
As the morning sun appears,
She wonders where the days have gone,
What's become of all the years.

NOTES: Whether introvert or extrovert, all of us engage in introspection now and again. This poem looks at the decisions people make or never make, and how action or inaction affects their lives. The final stanza reinforces the idea that indecision is time wasted that can't be returned. This topic is revisited in other works in this book. There was no model or inspiration for this work. It was solely from my imagination. It was an attempt to give voice and form to the concept of "Vacillation."

SUM OF YOUR PARTS

1st Verse:

Into my room comes Heidi Klum
That slender sweet and tremulous obsession.
Or is the sword you wield for Jessica Biel
Standing stark in shorts of compression?

Madge is my girl as her incarnations unfurl
Grinding down all our inhibitions.
Delightful and delirious, destructive and deciduous,
I really dig her exhibitions.

Chorus:

Forgive me, but where is your marathon?
What fuels your Grand Canyon ambition?
You got drawn into the game like that dude in Tron.
Now you must tear down the partition.

I love you baby, this you must know,
But unless I break through it's all for show.
If the whole is truly greater than the sum of your parts,
Then I think we've got something -- let's make a new start.

2nd Verse:

Megan Fox with my bagels and lox
On the morning after the fun.
This chick is so cool her feet make you drool,
When she beckons you jump up and run.

Charlize Theron with eyes that wear on
Every little thing that you do.
If she isn't Aphrodite, she's surely statuesque and mighty.
She reigns with a beauty that is regal and true.

Chorus:

Forgive me, but where is your marathon?
What fuels your Grand Canyon ambition?
You got drawn into the game like that dude in Tron.
Now you must tear down the partition.

I love you baby, this you must know,
But unless I break through it's all for show.
If the whole is truly greater than the sum of your parts,
Then I think we've got something -- let's make a new start.

Bridge:

I won't kid you -- I dig these chicks.
They take me where I really want to go.
But if you listen closely, you're in my heart mostly,
'Cause certain parts of them make the frame of your whole.

Thought I might call you on a Tuesday afternoon,
But you said you were busy and you'd call back soon.
Don't wait too long, there's a place in my heart.
Right here next to me I want the sum of your parts.

3rd Verse:

Pretty Katy Perry, she's a very sweet thing.
This chick has it all and her bird can sing.
Soft as a vesper, she knows how to play the game.
I've seen you in your zone -- baby you're the same.

Leona Lewis is smart and refined,
She's the picture of exquisite execution.
I can't get her face out of my mind,
So I'm begging you to give me absolution.

Alicia plays songs in the key of the heart.
Her melodies soar above the clouds.
Transcendent, resplendent, ethereal art,
Her spellbinding face is leonine and proud.

Scarlett Johansson, I held you for ransom
In a juicy little corner of my mind.
With an understated strut, you can really kick butt.
Your eyes are so sexy it's a crime.

2nd Bridge:

I know what to do when you call out my name,
But nothing gets done when you hammer on my brain.
You are all of these ladies rolled into one.
You are everything to me, why don't we have some fun?

Jonesing in January with Marisa Tomei,
I can't stop this obsession, but you can make it go away.
In my mind I see them all as their spirits laugh and call,
But when I see you all is quiet and I fall.

Outro:

Lovely Liz Hurley is not at all girly.
She's really all woman and more.
When she's waiting in a Bentley, you know she paid the rently.
If you're with her it's her legs you can't ignore.

Mila Kunis, feel the newness
Of a spanking fresh brand new day.
No simple affair; that's quite a derriere.
Her eyes pierce your soul and then she'll say

Chorus, repeat and fade:

© 2009, Michael A. Incitti

NOTES: Rap and Hip Hop are genres I don't usually work within. But this song came to me concurrently with the rhythms, which informed its structure. Driven by cadence and a heavy bass beat while the words came, it's clearly a rap song. The title came to me with the first two stanzas, and then it was off to the races writing as fast as I could. The work was inspired by word play and divergent thinking on a rainy summer evening. Like the rain outside the words kept coming.

GOODNIGHT IRENE

The arch of her foot,
Therein lies the source,
Of my pleasure, my pleasure divine.
The arch of her foot,
Where else but that nook,
Might my leisure, my leisure be shrined?

And of course, you say, 'Pray,
'Tell me how is it that you'
'Can pleasure derive from an arch?'
And I shall retort,
With a huff and a snort,
That you are a philistine tart.

Allow me at present
To somehow explain
My position regarding her ped.
An ingenuous dent --
Straps serve to accent,
Heels prattling – to these I am led.

While I reclined
A curious thought
Turned to words so benevolently said.
My darling, your taste
In fashion abates
One thousand fold when 'ere you wear Keds.

NOTES: I wrote this poem in the spring of 1979 at age 20. The title must have stayed in my memory from the old blues song of the same name, recorded by the Kingston Trio. The subject for it could have been any girl in a spring dress and high heels. Its purpose was to capture a moment. The words came to me and I just kept writing. There was no particular inspiration for this other than word play with sound, phrasing and meter. It is one my earliest poems as I worked to find a voice and to define my craft.

CHAPTER 2
I'LL WATCH OVER YOU

SOMETHING NEW

1st Verse: I know we just met,
But you're a woman of charm.
Let's go for a bite,
There's no need for alarm.

Too many people
Don't know what they're missin.'
We could have a lot of fun
Just talkin' and kissin.'

Sometimes I find
A girl who inspires.
Right now that's you,
But we must conspire

To find a moment or two
To say hello and goodbye.
I hope you don't forget
I'm captured by your eyes.

So if these lines of verse
Make you think of me,
Then these rhymes make sense
In the quest to make you see

That although we just met
And our moments are few,
I can honestly say,
Let's start something new.

Chorus:

Why don't we just start something new?
Forget the past – it's just us two.
Hold my hand, let's walk for a while.
I'll tell you some jokes and maybe make you smile.

When I look in your eyes there's no thought of forever.
When you whisper your sighs I know I'm not that clever.
Is it true what they say, we find love in a glance?
If that's how it goes let's start this romance.

Bridge:

Come with me,
Let's fly to Vegas.
One night or two
Won't make or break us.

Your laughter is my cue,
It's what I want to hear.
We've got something new,
There's more than what appears.

Chorus:

Why don't we just start something new?
Forget the past – it's just us two.
Hold my hand, let's walk for a while.
I'll tell you some jokes and maybe make you smile.

When I look in your eyes there's no thought of forever.
When you whisper your sighs I know I'm not that clever.
Is it true what they say, we find love in a glance?
If that's how it goes let's start this romance.

2nd Verse: Hollow eyes,
Vacant stare
Sittin' up high,
Walkin' on air.

Coin in the slot,
Pull the lever.
Pennies from heaven,
I'll leave you never.

Move to the table,
Pick up the dice.
This ain't no fable.
Winning is nice.

Drinking slow gin,
Night starts to fall.
Reach in my pocket
For a number I can call.

This place is a drag
'Cause it took all my money.
My spirit starts to sag
And the jokes aren't funny.

Wallet's getting lighter
And my chips are few.
I'm a lover not a fighter
And that's why I called you.

Chorus:

Repeat and close

NOTES: Word play and imagination fueled this story about a jet set romance between a guy and a girl who find their way to Las Vegas to have some fun. The staccato rhythm in the second verse matches the pace of the gambling tables.

MEETING OF THE MINDS

1st Verse:
Words can be your shield.
Words can be your plough.
Words can help you yield;
They simplify the now.

Talk with me,
What's on your mind?
Let me see,
And you may find.

We're not so far apart
That we can't find a way.
If you listen to your heart,
Then you will hear me say

Chorus:
It's a meeting of the minds
Tell me where you want to go.
We can talk and talk all night,
Tell me what you want to know.

This meeting of the minds,
It's not so hard to do.
Let your truths unwind,
To a consequence that's new.

1st Bridge:
Eat the bacon,
Leave the fat,
Live in nitrate city.
Rub your belly,
Grab your hat,
The morning isn't pretty.
Out the door
To greet the dawn.
Don't forget to put your rubbers on.
Another day
In revolving steel.
Isn't it time to just get real?

2nd Verse:
You said 'Talk is cheap
'And so are you.
'You won't pay the tab,
'Now your options are few.'

I said 'It's like you're in a movie
'You always make the scene.
'But you're never really there
'Until I hear you scream.'

'All your good intentions
'Go sliding out the door.
'All your silly pretensions
'Have me thinking. What for?'

You said 'I hate you with a passion
'Only love can understand.'
I said 'You make me crazy.
Now come and take my hand.'

Chorus:

2nd Bridge:
Don't fall for me,
I'm just passing through.
Temporary contract,
Unilateral and new.
I had a good sleep,
Once I finally fell.
Promises to keep,
And no lies to sell.
This is what I'm saying,
This is what I know.
Tomorrow we will laugh and play,
But now it's time to go.

3rd Verse:
The way you know what I'm thinking –
It's almost criminal.
Throw a lifeline when I'm sinking.
Your touch is subliminal.

My heart flutters
Each time you bat your eyes.
My camera has no shutters.
Please help me realize

You are not an illusion
In a diaphanous gown.
You're a canister of fusion
Exploding stars all around.

Chorus:

Minor Bridge:

Love you like thunder
Pounding in my brain.
Your sighs wash over me
Like a warm spring rain.

4th Verse: Out in the car
On a bright sunny day,
We hadn't gone far
When I heard you say,

This meeting of the minds
It's not so hard to do.
So you don't get left behind
Maybe you should try it too.

Chorus:

NOTES: This was written on multiple days in spring and summer in 2010.
Inspiration came from multiple sources creating sense impressions unified
by a central theme, and driven by internal rhythm.

I'LL WATCH OVER YOU

1st Verse:

I'll watch over you, yes
I'll watch over you,
Until the sun lights up the sky,
And it shines.

I'll watch over you, yes,
I'll watch over you,
Until the night becomes the day,
And we play.

Chorus:

I love you so.
My heart's aglow.
I'll watch over you, yes
I'll watch over you tonight.
'Till morning comes,
I will be by your side all night.
I'll make the darkness fade from sight.
All that I ask is please, please
Just come back to me,
Come back to me.
It's as if you've never gone.
Oh, come back to me.
Come back to me,
My beautiful child.

2nd Verse:

I'll watch over you, yes
I'll watch over you,
Until the stars above align,
'Cause you're mine.

I'll watch over you, yes
I'll watch over you,
No matter what you do or say,
That's my way.

Chorus:

Bridge:

Suddenly the morning comes.
The night has gone away.
Now our lives have just begun.
We bow our heads and pray.
Pray for another blessed day.
Pray for the love of God always.
Lift your voice to the sky.
God's love will shine above all.
Listen and you'll hear His call.

3rd Verse:

I'll watch over you, yes
I'll watch over you,
Although your life's in disarray,
Come what may.

I'll watch over you, yes
I'll watch over you,
Until the oceans all run dry,
Don't you cry.

Chorus:

Instrumental close:

© 2011, 2015, Michael A. Incitti

NOTES: This was originally written in December 2010 for a coffee commercial contest. I wrote a story about a girl caring for her dog through the night. The dog got better as morning came. I wrote the music to it, and expanded the verses from what started as a 30-second spot to what is now a bright and uplifting 3-minute song. I added the bridge in April 2015. It's a nice Christian song in C major with a B minor bridge.

IN THE MOMENT COMPLETE

Chorus:

Tony rode shotgun, cigarette in hand.
Eddie drove his red 'Vette like a wave on the sand.
Two friends cruisin' in the moment complete.
Nothin' else mattered 'cept the ground beneath their feet.

1st Verse:

Eddie was fast.
Eddie was cool.
Played him some hoops,
He was nobody's fool.

Lived in the penthouse,
Got a full ride.
No time to study,
Nowhere to hide.

Livin' large on campus,
Party at the frat.
'Profs don't know nothin.'
'I coulda told ya that.'

Eddie had game,
Moved the ball with speed.
But the coach sat him down
Cause the rules he did not heed.

Chorus:

Tony rode shotgun, cigarette in hand.
Eddie drove his red 'Vette like a wave on the sand.
Two friends cruisin' in the moment complete.
Nothin' else mattered 'cept the ground beneath their feet.

2nd Verse:

Tony tried to focus
But he just couldn't study.
Said 'The joke's on you,
Gonna hang with my buddy.'

So Tony said to Eddie
'Let's cruise in your car.
That's a fine set of wheels,
You must be a star.'

Eddie said 'I used to be a star.
'But they took away my place.
'Now I gotta make some money
'Just to save face.'

So Tony said to Eddie,
'I know what you can do.
'There's a dude down the street
'Who's just lookin' for you.'

Chorus:

Tony rode shotgun, cigarette in hand.
Eddie drove his red 'Vette like a wave on the sand.
Two friends cruisin', in the moment complete.
Nothin' else mattered 'cept the ground beneath their feet.

3rd Verse:

Eddie was fast.
Eddie was cool.
Smoked him some grass,
He was nobody's fool.

Eddie got wise,
Learned how they moved the stuff.
He wouldn't listen to advice.
Said he'd seen and heard enough.

Tony said 'Looky here.
'You gotta give 'em their cut.
'If they find you keepin' it all
'They gonna crack you like a nut.'
Just then a car pulled up alongside
And put a dent in Eddie's 'Vette.
'Hey what the hell you doin,' man?
'Don't you know I'll pay the rest?'

Chorus:

Tony rode shotgun, cigarette in hand.
Eddie drove his red 'Vette like a wave on the sand.
Two friends cruisin', in the moment complete.
Nothin' else mattered 'cept the ground beneath their feet.

4th Verse:

That dude from the street rolled his tinted window down.
He had a crocodile smile that masqueraded as a frown.
The red light turned green, but neither car moved.
You could tell that the dude had something to prove.

'Where's my cash, Crazy Eddie?
'You know you can't get ahead.
'You're gonna pay me, chump,
'Until you cold and dead.'

Eddie was afraid, and Tony sat still.
Neither knew what to say, and they both felt a chill.
Finally Eddie said 'Just gimme a chance to pay.
'The money's in my room, you can have it any day.'

The dude waved a piece and then he said real shrewd,
'That might work for someone else, but to me it's just plain rude.
'I'll tell you what you can do, you can give me your Corvette.'
Eddie said 'That ain't gonna happen. That's something I'd regret.'

Instrumental Bridge:

5th Verse:

No one heard the gunshots,
That echoed from the streets.
No one saw the car that sped away,
Tires screeching its retreat.
No one knew the bodies
That in the front seats lay.
Just two guys out on the town,
But their skin was cold and gray.

The police called the college,
Said we have a few of yours.
The college said 'Oh no you don't,
'We kicked them out two weeks before.'

A couple of girls were walking downtown
And they happened by the scene.
'Hey isn't that Eddie's 'Vette?' one said.
'No way,' said the other. 'It couldn't be.'

Chorus:

Tony rode shotgun, cigarette in hand.
Eddie drove his red 'Vette like a wave on the sand.
Two friends cruisin', in the moment complete.
Nothin' else mattered 'cept the ground beneath their feet.

NOTES: I wrote the chorus in the car at a red light in mid-October 2010 while on my way to a soccer game. Two high school kids pulled up alongside my car. The kid riding shotgun was smoking and trying to look cool. The four-line stanza came to me immediately. I scribbled it on a notepad. The light turned green and I drove on to my game. A few days later two stanzas came to me. Then months went by and nothing. On May 9, 2011, midnight to 2:21 a.m., I finished it. Once I knew how the characters' story would end, the stanzas came to me in a flash. I could see the words very clearly in my mind, line by line. I chose "In the Moment Complete" as the title because that moment in the car while they were riding together and having fun was all they ever had.

THE VISIT

Memories of the past had gathered in my mind,
And I resolved to visit her one last time.
How long has it been? Five years and more.
Will she remember me, or will she seem unsure?

Golden blonde hair, soft as a dove.
Eyes of China blue, radiating love.
Soft ruby lips, a warm, feline smile.
Colt-like legs, moving all the while.

Do my memories deceive me?
Were you once unkind?
We remember the best,
And to the rest we are blind.

Ah, but I remember the time we shared.
Though brief as a candle there was no doubt we cared.
We walked hand-in-hand through evenings in the snow,
Then we held each other close before the fire's glow.
We rode makeshift sleds down hills of ice –
Inexperienced players in a game of dice.

Now I drive to see her
In the clear country where
The sun is out, and spring abounds,
But there's a chilling stillness in the air.

I see her house 'neath Douglas firs
Hidden behind an inn.
I pause a moment to think of what to say,
Then, with abandon, I begin.

A plodding old woman came to the door.
Disheveled by sleep, she looked somewhat forlorn.
"Is Susie here? We were friends once, you know."
She shook her head and said, "She and her mother
moved away long ago."

A familiar pain lodged in my throat;
My eyes fought back the tears.
How could I have been such a sentimental fool?
There was little comfort in the passage of years.

The sun shone so brilliantly,
And the trees and flowers bloomed.
But on this day I found a love long gone.
I closed to the door to one of my heart's rooms.

NOTES: I wrote this piece in spring 1985 while I was working, teaching, and going to school at night at Temple University in Philadelphia. This lyric poem came from an attempt at collaboration when I answered an ad for a lyricist posted in the music department at Temple. Unfortunately the pianist/composer, while an earnest and pleasant woman, was very nearly tone deaf. So my words stand alone, for now. Once I chose the subject for the song, I took a drive in the countryside of Blue Bell to get visual ideas for the setting. The rest is my imagination.

SUMMER NIGHTS

The feminine night force marches in the alleyway below.
Their coming is signaled by the hollow cow-bell plock of
red and white high heels on cobblestone.
The march comes at midnight and beyond.
These girls are young, in their late teens.
Their hair is long, their bodies tight.
Short tight shorts and halter tops leave little to the imagination.
I am roused from sleep, you see, compelled to rise in the
summer night,
As touched by Calliope's verse, and Circe's call.

From my second-story window I hear them walking.
The plocking sound echoes in cadence through the canyons of
row homes, and
Punctuates their voices, hushed in a dulcet tremolo.
It is a lonely, desolate, harsh, mocking call to the mortals who
people mundane worlds.
Only young girls truly inhabit the summer night.
They embrace it like a lover, oblivious to Morpheus' lure.
For Night is the little brother of Death; he calls the young girls
out of their homes with a sweet promise of surrender
Beneath a violet, starry shroud of passion, and the freedom it
releases.

On this night one girl smokes through the lingering mist of a
quiet summer rain.
A tiny orange circle glows inches from her soft young lips,
Like a lantern preceding and illuminating her blonde hair.
Suddenly the circle of orange becomes intense and aflame;
Just as suddenly, it relaxes and recedes with her silent exhale.
The atoms of her sigh are scattered in the consenting night air.
Her secrets intact, she casts the cigarette into a puddle of rainwater.
She slips away with her friends silent as a cat; she and the night are one.

NOTES: "Summer Nights" was written in 15 minutes on 5-21-85, at 9:30 p.m., and 5-22-85, at 8:45 a.m., in our 2nd floor apartment amid the row homes in the Castor Gardens section of Northeast Philadelphia. I generally don't like free verse. It doesn't lend itself well to musical accompaniment. But I included this work for its evocative use of language. Even the great poet Robert Frost was not a fan of free verse: "I would as soon write free verse as I would play tennis with the net down." This work won an honorable mention in a poetry contest I entered that same year. "Summer Nights" reflected an intense moment of awareness and observation, which, I suppose, is a cornerstone of writing poetry. Thematically it reminded me of the Mama's and the Papa's song, "Twelve-Thirty: Young Girls Are Coming to the Canyon," by composer John Phillips. I wrote the first two 8-line stanzas in 10 minutes the night before. Next morning I awoke with an image in my mind of a young girl smoking a cigarette in the alley between the row homes. The line "The atoms of her sigh are scattered in the consenting night air" is pretty powerful and almost it captures the entire work's mood and theme. I wrote the last stanza in five minutes, just describing what I saw in my mind's eye. Plock is a beautiful city in Poland, but the adjective "plocking" doesn't exist. I coined the word to describe the sound of the girls' wood-soled sandals on the concrete echoing off the brick and fieldstone walls of the row homes. It is an example of onomatopoeia, a word that sounds like what it's describing. Don't ask me to spell that again. Generally, I like a defined rhythm and structure, but free verse gave me a lot of room here. And I used it.

EL CASINO REEL
(LAS VEGAS IMPRESSIONS)

The quintet seated at the table of Jack
Proved an interesting study in cool.
Though long after they've gone the cards will flow on,
Life through the corner of one's eye is the rule.

Two hippies from yesteryear retained their cynical guise.
A mini-riot had just begun – the result of words unwise.
The hippies were guilty and all were willing
To pelt them to death with dice.

Two gamblers entered the dining hall
Poker-faced and steady as rocks.
But upon reaching the line found they didn't have time
And, flustered, they left tugging their socks.

Two stars and their entourage
Graced the two a.m. buffet.
They refused to sit down and left with frowns –
The lights were too dim for their taste.

Two tourists searched, but could not find
The illustrious dining hall.
But after checking their wallets and their empty pockets
Found they weren't that hungry after all.

Two swingers glittered their way
To the dining room so as to sup.
Their clothes were so tight they looked a fright.
They choked on their smoke and threw up.

Two men who were six-foot-ten stuffed themselves
At the two a.m. buffet.
In silence they ate 'till the food trays were empty,
And then they wobbled away.

NOTES: I wrote this piece in June 1979 at age 20, while visiting Las Vegas on a trip west with my family. I always had a note pad with me to record thoughts, ideas, and unusual occurrences. I'd be called a nerd today, but as a writer, it was something I had to do. The title is a play on the word "Reel" as in 'a reel of film.' One month later I wrote "Perspective," and a month after that I wrote the lyrics for "Manhattan Skyline." Both works were significant leaps forward for me as I continued to develop my craft. In addition to the notes that produced the above work, I played blackjack in Vegas and won.

We drove cross country on that trip to Las Vegas. I had never really been anywhere other than the 1964 World's Fair in New York City as a child, and the suburbs of New Jersey to visit relatives. So Vegas was cool. I looked older than 20 with my beard – one of my aunts said I was a wooly individual, whereupon I broke into a verse of "Wooly Bully." So no one questioned me when I sat down to gamble at the blackjack tables. I won a few hundred dollars, then I took one of my cousins to the midnight buffet for steak, ribs, chicken and lobster. She talked while I listened and people-watched, absorbed by the scenes in front of me. Next day my parents and aunts and uncles went to see the showgirls. But I used my winnings to buy a ticket to see Glen Campbell play the songs of the great songwriter, Jimmy Webb. Campbell is one of the legendary country and pop singers and guitarists of our time. Propelled by the music of master composer Webb, it was a musical match made in heaven. The power of the music and the electricity in the room were incredible. I sat at a round table midway from the stage, surrounded by people 30 to 40 years older than me, listening to music that I had only previously heard on the radio. For a kid who had never been anywhere, it was fascinating to see the effect that great music had on a live audience.

THE OTHER SIDE OF PARADISE

We surround ourselves in college days
With mirror reflections for friends.
Sharing identical, cynical views
Toward the parade of fools without end.

Mirth comes quickly and easily,
Compared to the business of thought.
All seems trite and absurd, you know,
A dubious battle to be fought.

But soon war's toll weighs heavy,
Roads part as pragmatism calls.
Days at once rich with folly and growth
Were rehearsals for strides and falls.

The other side to the paradise we knew
Held faraway eyes laughing and blue.
A moment to pause and reflect on those days –
The girls in spring dresses, the warm summer haze.

Time fleeting, pressing onward through the night,
Careening like spirits of rage in flight.
Then splendor and peace serene as a fawn
Flower in the wind of an amber dawn.

© 1982, 2012, Michael A. Incitti

NOTES: I wrote this poem in 1982 while working at the Grit Sunday newspaper and national magazine. They had some space to fill in the same issue in which I had written a feature interview on the great songwriter Paul Williams, ("We've Only Just Begun," and more, with Roger Nichols). Paul is now the president of ASCAP, the American Society of Composers and Publishers. Mr. Williams did not see my poem in that issue, at least he and his publicist never mentioned it when they called back the next week to say thank you for the glowing article. I wrote this on a typewriter in 30 minutes just ahead of a deadline. The night editor resembled the legendary journalist H.L. Mencken, with bushy eyebrows and Coke bottle glasses. He smoked a cigar in the news room. I handed the poem to him and he asked where I got the title. I said it was a play on the F. Scott Fitzgerald title "This Side of Paradise." He exhaled smoke and walked away. An hour later he showed me the page proof and said, "Not bad, kid."

WHEN WE LOVE

If there was a way
To step back into time,
I'd go back to the day
When you were mine.
Freedom was ours,
And happiness and dreams.
And a love so right
Nothing would change, it seemed.
Please tell me why
All good things must end?
And why do we long
For those times again?
My brothers and sisters
And their kids have grown old.
Years pass so fast,
But slowly they show that
When we love,
Time waits forever.
Maybe in heaven
We'll again be together.

The times that defined
The life that we knew
Came with Kodak moments
In number too few.
Now all that's left
Is a picture book.
But the mem'ries prevent me
From taking a look.

© 1979, 2011, Michael A. Incitti

NOTES: My mother's side of the family included 7 kids which gave me 4 aunts, 3 uncles, and numerous cousins. To borrow from "The Godfather," if my Mom was the *consigliere* of the family, my Aunt Mary was the godfather, or godmother, as it were. And I was her favorite nephew. She lost her first husband at a relatively young age. He was the love of her life, and these were her words to me, in poetic form, describing their love.

THE GEOMETRY OF LOVE

1ˢᵗ Verse:

Hearts get broken every day,
It's a fact you can't ignore.
One wants to leave while the other one stays,
And he walks right out the door.

You and I, we've been down that road,
We've walked that lonely mile.
Angry days and restless nights intersect
In search of a parallel smile.

Chorus:

The geometry of love is an incongruent angle.
It occurs at any point on a grid.
The geometry of love knows no rhyme or reason.
And it doesn't really care what you did.

The geometry of love is a time without a season
Existing on a plane of its own.
The geometry of love cannot be bartered.
It will never be the object of a loan.

2ⁿᵈ Verse:

Joyce thought she had a husband.
They lived together for a very long time.
But her lines were straight and his were scattered.
He played guitar in the moonlight sublime.

He started a band and they played a lot of oldies --
Eagles, Glen Campbell, and the King.
He never understood why she always came around.
She just wanted to hear him sing.

Chorus:

Bridge:

We go through our days in a circular maze
Searching for a congruent heart.
We put our best face forward as we move along the edge
Taking care to always play our part.

But this is what you get, you get caught in a net
That surrounds the borders of your mind.
You're trapped by fear with coordinates unclear.
Your own reflection won't let you unwind.

3rd Verse:

Dorothy thought she had it all,
Thirty years with a man named Ben.
He was her lover, he was her life,
He was always her very best friend.

A life in the suburbs, two kids and a dog,
By day an electrical engineer.
But the spark was long gone. At night he sang sad songs.
When morning came it was perfectly clear.

Chorus:

Repeat 1st Verse, Chorus, and Close

NOTES: On March 25, 2014, I returned a cassette tape recorder to an electronics store. There were few people in the store, so the clerk, Joyce, talked about her life. As one who is a good listener, sometimes people just like to talk to me. Minutes later I went to another store to buy a card for a friend. Another clerk, an older woman with a Brooklyn accent who was quite talkative, told me about her life. This was Dorothy. Joyce's story is fairly direct, but Dorothy's has some literary license. Both character's names are fictional. The next morning when I woke up the first four lines of this poem were in my head. I sat down and started writing and the rest followed almost verbatim.

JOANNE

Joanne we can't go on this way.
It's a sin to believe there is nothing to say.
A man will do things that he don't understand,
And he'll try not to think of forgotten plans.
He'll slave through the day and tread home at night.
And he'll wonder about his God-awful plight.
But when he walks through the door and he tracks up the floor
With the pain and the sweat from his singular war,
It's good to know there's a woman at home
Who still loves him despite all the faded photos of
fragmented smiles lined and creased long ago.
Joanne we can't go on this way.
It's a sin to believe there is nothing to say.

I know you well, but do you know me?
If you did you would surely see.
You'd see a light has faded from my eyes.
The weight of the years is a sad lullaby.
We all come from somewhere; we all have a place to be.
We look into each other's eyes, yet we refuse to see.
How can we call it love when it doesn't even rhyme?
How can we say it's beautiful when you just don't have the time?
How can we dream of tomorrow when we can't always live for today?
How can I save you the sorrow when your fears I cannot allay?
Joanne we can't go on this way.
It's a sin to believe there is nothing to say.

© 1979, 2011, Michael A. Incitti

NOTES: I wrote this poem in the spring of 1979. It came to me in one 10-minute burst. While in college a friend of mine and I had a Simon and Garfunkel-type act. He played guitar and I sang. We had a gig for a party at the house of a professor. I hadn't eaten all day, so on a break I was in a corner getting cozy with a pizza. In the hallway beyond, a conversation took place between the professor and her husband. This poem was inspired somewhat by what I overheard. But it was largely driven by rhythm and an assortment of images and sense impressions. "Joanne," not her real name, had long blonde hair. She wore a Kelly-green dress and high heels. She did not look the part of a professor. Because they had a good crowd, my buddy and I extended our set by an hour to get a nice tip. To paraphrase Harry Chapin's song "Taxi," we stashed a C-note in our shirts, then we left.

CHAPTER 3
ONE CHILD SAVED

USE ME AGAIN

She was like the morning sun,
Fresh and clean and new.
I saw her once and made her mine.
No one else would do.

We lived together in a two-room flat.
Each day we walked to the beach.
We shared a towel beneath a turquoise sky.
Our hands were always in reach.

She wondered if our love would last.
I said I know it will.
God chose us to live as one,
While others were searching still.

The days went by, the nights grew cold
And the ocean sang its song.
She woke one morning with a smile that held a secret.
Said we'd be three before long.

Then one day I came home from work
A neighbor walked toward me in a hurry.
'The ambulance came and took her away,
She didn't want you to worry.'

I rushed to the hospital and ran to her room.
I prayed 'Please God, let her be OK.'
Her tanned skin was pale and her hair wet with sweat.
There were no words to say.

I held her close as she awoke and
Told her everything will be fine.
She asked 'Is she all right, our baby girl?'
'Honey you did great.' But I didn't know if I had lied.

Then she closed her eyes and whispered
'I used you for everything, my strength, my love, my light. '
'Get some rest now, my love,' I said.
'Soon it will be night.'

The doctor and nurses came rushing in.
I knew something was wrong.
Her tired body would not respond.
With tears in her eyes a nurse said, 'She's gone.'

Fifteen summers rolled by like waves,
But I know she's still by my side.
When I see our little girl run on the beach,
I know her mother's spirit will abide.

I begged and bartered and pleaded with God,
Could I have her for just one more day?
Let her use me again to live, to laugh and love.
This can't be Your way?

But God had no answer,
Least none that I could see.
And then one night soon after,
My wife came to me in a dream.

She said, 'God has a plan
That none of us can know.
You just have to keep on living,
And help our little girl grow.'

'You have to believe
That in living every day
You are doing God's bidding,
You are keeping God's way.'

'I know it's hard, my love,
But please don't grieve.
I feel it in your heart,
But it was just my time to leave.'

'I'll wait for an eternity
That we can share together.
My love for you will last,
I will leave you never.'

For the first time in a long time
I slept peacefully and deep.
The image of her face was locked in my mind.
The beauty of her heart I'll always keep.

Twenty more years have come and gone,
And I think about her still.
She's with me every day, in our daughter's work and play.
My love for her remains, and somewhere, somehow, she knows it always
will.

Friends say I should find another woman,
Said maybe I could try and pretend.
But I know in this world, for me there's no other girl.
I want the one I love to use me all over again.

NOTES: I wrote this poem in an hour from 11 a.m. to noon on 9-4-12 at
Barnes and Noble in Wilkes-Barre, Pa., after writing "Island Blue," also in
chapter 3, and another poem an hour before. I wrote it in my mind while
driving in the car. Then I stopped at the book store and wrote it completely
on my legal pad while sitting in the coffee shop. These ideas appeared and
demanded to be written. There were no immediate visual images or pure
inspirations; they were just words to a story that came to me. But as the
story came through I used my imagination to attach visual images to drive
the narrative forward. The subject was clearly, as Wordsworth said, "a
spontaneous overflow of powerful emotion."

THIS DANCE

She drives him wild,
He fills her mind.
It's her number that he dials,
But she hangs up all the time.

He tried to let her go
But she would not leave.
She said they're stuck together,
And there will be no reprieve.

It doesn't sound right
And it doesn't make sense.
It's a lie, it's a fake
And it won't pay the rent.

What's your name, what's your game?
Her face says trouble.
His mind says one thing
But her body says another.

It's not about me, he said,
It's all about you.
You need to get away
From the person you knew.

Do you tell me lies, she said,
Because they sound better?
Or do you lie to yourself
Because it's easy to remember?

She said sometimes what you want
Never really comes around.
But what you don't expect
Brings your feet back to the ground.

He said thousands of people,
They come and they go.
You meet one special girl,
Somehow both of you know.

He'd drive a thousand miles,
Then he'd drive a thousand more
To be with her an hour.
That's what he's living for.

We try to live in the moment,
We strive to seize the day.
We set out to capture some scenes of rapture
Before we're called in from our play.

Life can be a gamble.
Life can be a bet.
You can count your winnings
If your wallet's with you yet.

He held her heart
In the palm of his hand.
She kept on forgetting
To put her feet on dry land.

But now she is with him
Every hour of every day.
Sometimes there is candy,
Sometimes a bright bouquet.

He brings her rain and flowers in the spring.
She brings him snowflakes and a catchy song to sing.
They cherish every moment as if it were their last.
Their trials are never over, but they keep them in the past.

NOTES: This began as an attempt to write a song for a movie, but it took on a direction of its own on its way to equilibrium. I wrote it in an hour after watching the movie, "Love and Other Drugs." My primary goal was to capture the rhythm and pace of the dialogue. The interplay of the main characters – actors Anne Hathaway and Jake Gyllenhaal -- had the effect of a dance or a tennis match, even though they never set foot on a dance floor or a tennis court.

BEST FRIENDS

Johnny's sleeping things are quiet for a while,
When he wakes it's a hurricane of fun.
He throws my ball and I fetch it back
And I smile with my eyes, see how we run.

You and I are best of friends.
That's how it will always be.
Our bond as one will never end.
Our den will transcend all we can see.

Chorus:

I'll be watching you all night,
While you dream of days to come.
Keeping close 'till morning light,
Running in an endless summer sun.

2nd Verse:

Growing old is a fact we both must face
But for now, we're together, just you and me.
Sad to say that someday, we may be apart,
But we'll be together again, as far as we both can see.

We share a love that comes only once
In a life that always looks for more.
I'll be your friend and watch over you
And you'll give me the love that I adore.

Chorus:

I'll be watching you all night,
While you dream of days to come.
Keeping close 'till morning light,
We'll escape and find the sun.

3rd Verse:
My life by design will be shorter than yours,
A dog knows that from the start.
We are loving angels placed here by God
To tend the human heart.

Our time has a touch of the eternal.
In your memory I will always live.
No matter what happens, no matter where you go,
My love and protection I will always give.

Chorus:

I'll be watching you all night
While you dream of days to come.
Keeping close till morning light,
Running in an endless summer sun.

NOTES: I wrote this in 1982 while I was a newspaper reporter at The Grit. A photo came over the news wire of a German shepherd sitting on a couch watching a little boy who was asleep on the couch next to him. It occurred to me to write lyrics to the photo, and, with the tune of Billy Joel's "Say Goodbye to Hollywood" in mind for rhythm, I wrote this poem from the viewpoint of what the dog might have to say to the boy if he could talk. On slow news days, or when my assigned duties were complete, I would assign myself this exercise, pulling wire photos and writing from what I saw. It was good training to take a visual image and give it an identity that could be set to music.

I've had dogs since I was 8 years old. Here is my best friend, Mickey, every bit a Jack Russell terrier, full of energy and ready to investigate anything. I adopted him from the local SPCA. He was returned by someone after less than a year because he had a snaggle tooth and therefore could not be a show dog. I don't know what any of that means, but he was good enough for me. He's 3 years old in this photo, and as of this writing he's 9 and going strong. The photo was taken by my wife, Aprile.

BEST FRIENDS II

She's walkin' down the lane with her kitty on her shoulder,
Such a fine day – spring couldn't be bolder.
She's got plans that Momma won't believe.
Out into the fields where the blossoms are growing,
Folks don't seem to see what she's showing,
Her friends will all be there – she just can't wait to leave.

Chorus:

In the bright sunshine
Everything is warm and rosy.
In that mornin' light
Life is sweet and fresh and cozy.
There's her special friend,
Hey Momma it's not 'bye bye,'
It's just puppy love,
We all have to start out some time.

Now school's a drag – she stares out the window
Waitin' for the bell and watchin' the wind blow,
Rustlin' her dreams like a whirlwind on the plain.
That boy sits beside her passin' notes and laughin'
Teacher blames her – she don't know what happened.
The boy just smiles and says 'Amy I can hardly wait.'

Chorus:

In the bright sunshine
Everything is warm and rosy.
In that mornin' light
Life is sweet and fresh and cozy.
There's her special friend.
Hey Momma it's not 'bye bye,'
It's just puppy love
We all have to start out some time.

NOTES: "Best Friends II" was another writing exercise on a slow news day in 1982. The story was based on a wire photo of a little girl walking down a country road on a sunny day with a kitten wrapped in a handkerchief and hanging on a stick over her shoulder. I wrote this 3rd person lyric to the tune of Dolly Parton's song, "9 to 5."

Our other best friend was Rachel, a black lab and German Shepherd mix. She was very protective of the kids, especially near a swimming pool. She loved the water, but she loved snow even more. The most graceful dog I've ever seen, Rachel galloped like a horse. Here, Rachel keeps an eye on her charges, our daughter Chelsea, our son Marc, and our daughter Marissa, the book publisher.

ONE CHILD SAVED

Can somebody tell me why there are wars?
And why people are locked in without any doors?
Why do horror, hatred and poverty prevail
Over kindness and love, and warm soothing gales?

Where are my friends who once ran in the streets?
Their gardens are empty as they die in the heat.
The rocks are so cold and pointed and cruel.
Will all of our suffering end in this duel?

Or will we fight a battle in a struggle for self,
Reaching deep within while outside lies help?
What makes a war and who's to decide
How young men, women and children should die?

Diana, she tried to save us from hate.
She tried to remove the weapons of destruction.
She couldn't do it alone, she was so far from home,
And how could she without any instruction?

I've so many questions,
There's much I don't know.
But will I be able to play?
Will I be able to grow?

A great man once said that one child saved
Is worth more than a thousand slain foes.
In the eyes of God I know that it's true.
But the enemy still haunts from below.

If I could wave my hand
And protect all at my command,
I'd take away the bombs and the tanks and the guns,
And I'd keep everyone safe until there were none.

I've so many questions –
I know I'm quite young.
But will my life be over
Before it's begun?

NOTES: I began writing this poem in the spring of 1982 at my desk in the Grit news room late on a Saturday night after I finished the police news. I came across an AP news wire photo that depicted a boy of maybe age 7 or 8 playing outdoors on a rocky ledge wearing a plastic Army helmet and holding a toy machine gun. But the look on his face was one of wonder and uncertainty rather than aggression. It reminded me that most soldiers in battle are, with few exceptions, reluctant participants. Now imagine a little boy who is exposed to war. What would he say about it? So this poem is the internal monologue of an articulate and peaceful child who does not want to be in harm's way. I like to believe that all of us are capable of choosing peace and development rather than war and destruction. I added the reference to Princess Diana of Wales in 2012 prior to copyrighting the work. She worked tirelessly to help innocent children who were badly injured by land mines. Diana died far too young, but her legacy of peace, love and charity for all lives on in her sons, William and Harry. She is still an inspiration to the world, not just to Great Britain. This poem is a tribute to Diana and to her humanitarian works. The reference to the great man's quote was that of William Faulkner in his acceptance speech for the Nobel Prize in literature, which he won in 1949. One of the great American novelists who epitomized the era of Realism and Naturalism, Faulkner's masterpiece, "The Sound and the Fury," was always one of my favorites.

SIDEBAR: After nearly a century of operation, The Grit was bought out in the spring of 1983. It suffered significant layoffs and personnel changes at its home office in Williamsport, Pa. For a time editorial operations ceased as it re-invented itself to align with its new owner. I secured a position with a daily newspaper to the south. At its peak The Grit had a circulation of more than 1 million across rural America. It was a slice of small-town Americana. In literature I can think of only one analog and that was Sherwood Anderson's classic work, "Winesburg, Ohio," depicting characters in a fictional rural town through the eyes of its protagonist, George Willard, a reporter for the Winesburg Eagle. "Winesburg, Ohio" is one of my favorite books, and it presents some of the most vivid character portraits in all of literature.

ISLAND BLUE

Chorus:

Island blue, island blue, what have they done to you?
Island blue, island blue, how could this be true?
The machinery of progress has destroyed the land.
Man's forward movement came with a heavy hand.
Our ancestors cared for the Earth to its core.
We reap what we sow, a living planet no more.

1st Verse:

Today my eyes were opened, though seeing from afar.
The beauty that you used to be has exploded like a star.
Why does man continue as his own worst enemy?
All the while the rank and file struggle to be free.

Chorus:

Bridge:

I see you in the moonlight,
A silent orbit through the night.
Beneath a starlit canopy,
We struggle to find entropy.
In the dawn of a new day
We light the vision of a new way.
The noise of war will cease,
A galaxy at peace.

2nd Verse:

Empires have risen from the Earth's nascent crust.
But by decree man's history reduces them to dust.
When will we begin to see the futility of hate?
As long as man's alive, my friend, it cannot be too late.

Chorus:

Bridge:

Mother Earth in all her glory
Turns away from the red planet's fury.
A sea of tranquility bathes the rising sun.
We will return to her when our days are done.

Chorus:

Epilogue:

We are but a moment on this island of earth and sand.
Our fleeting days like the rush of waves are the touch of a loving hand.
We must learn to protect our world, to keep her safe from sorrow.
Because if we lie the price is high; there may not be a tomorrow.

NOTES: Some of the stanzas for "Island Blue" were written in 2010 with the entire work completed in spring 2012. This is an anti-war song, and an ecology song written as commentary against fracking, which has destroyed landscapes and threatened farmlands, livestock and water supplies in search of natural gas. The anti-war element is in keeping with the overall theme of One Child Saved. The war within this framework refers to our battle to save our planet ecologically, and to address man's inhumanity to man, wherever it may occur on the globe. Thus far, I'm the only writer I know who can rhyme canopy with entropy* and get away with it. OK, maybe not.

*Entropy is a term from physics that generally refers to multiple routes or systems which lead to the same end, as in the Second Law of Thermodynamics. The reference underscores the irreversibility of processes both natural and unnatural that occur on the Earth, and the asymmetry between the past and the future that results.

HARLOT'S TRILOGY

Perspective

The portrait of her face is painted and framed
Upon the walls that surround my mind.
I stand in the middle of my gallery,
Admiring the beauty of my find.

Through brushstrokes applied with meticulous ease
Indeed, I sigh, she's one of a kind.
And then I realize, like an artist's dream,
I'd see her if I were blind.

Performance

She comes out of the night and makes the pain go away.
Such a heavenly sight, you'll ask her to stay.
Her touch is warm, her sigh so real,
A statuesque form, a Venus to feel.

Who is this enchantress whose emotions are sealed?
An actress who can't miss, at the altar of lust she kneels.
When morning comes you're once again whole.
You've paid the sum for a human soul.

Penance

Happiness, a forgotten thing, waits at the window, a bird who can't sing.
Outside the wind blows on a night cold and wet. She wonders if her
friends are waiting for her yet.
Outrageous imagery careens through her mind, ghosts of fantasy
rollicking purblind.
She opens the door to the sound of a bell; an icy gale enters with
a calling card from hell.

Somewhere there is laughter.
Somewhere there is light.
Somewhere there is humanity,
But she has come to fear the night.

© 1979, 2011, Michael A. Incitti

NOTES: I wrote Perspective in July 1979, the summer before my senior year at Bloomsburg. I was taking classes, working at a downtown restaurant and lifeguarding at a campus pool. I had a cousin who also attended Bloomsburg. She was a year younger and grew up next door to me. She and a girlfriend of hers who owned a Husky visited me at my apartment. I gave them iced tea and pretzels, then I had to get to work at the restaurant downtown, so they left. When I came back I turned on a desk lamp I kept at a small table – the only light in the room -- got out my legal pad, and wrote the eight lines to "Perspective" verbatim. There were no accompanying images as I wrote. I saw only the words in my mind's eye. To this day I don't know where those words came from. Everything I wrote I did on my own, largely self-taught, and completely self-motivated. These expressions in literary form were driven by forces in me that I can't pinpoint other than a strong desire to communicate thoughts and ideas. One thing I learned from many literary sources was that a writer must be true to himself at all times, and he must be true to what he writes.

In August 1984, after five years of writing for newspapers in Pennsylvania, I was accepted for graduate school in journalism at Temple University in Philadelphia. I completed the degree in 3 semesters while teaching part-time on campus during the day and working full-time at night on a suburban newspaper. In early spring 1985 I wrote one of the best feature stories I'd ever written in terms of content, tone, tempo, diction, and structure. The piece was on a high-priced call girl who lived in a condo in the Philadelphia suburbs. She was lovely. A Jewish woman in her mid to late 30s, she played piano, had strawberry-blonde hair, wire rim glasses, and a voluptuous body. She was well-read, fluent in several languages, and one could easily picture her accompanying any man anywhere, from dignitaries and politicos to rock stars and sports figures. The assignment was to write something people would be compelled to read. I figured sex sells, so why not? We got the entire 3-hour interview done in one cold March night, and as one who was working 3 jobs at the time, I greatly appreciated that she didn't charge me a nickel. While writing the story the poems Performance and Penance came to me. I combined the three short poems in succession – Perspective, Performance, Penance – for the present compilation, but each functioned as the lead to introduce subsections of the feature story. The instructor, a Pulitzer Prize winning journalist from the Philadelphia Inquirer, Jonathan Neumann, loved the story and the accompanying verse. My idea prompted a similar assignment at the Inquirer. I got an A for my work and for the course, but I didn't get a job at the Inquirer.

WHAT A TEAM YOU'VE GOT

1st Verse:

Jordan you've got hands of gold
You smash the ball
And then you're bold to them,
You're quite a gem.
Kayla skies above the net
She spikes the ball
Until we get our wins
Do it again.

Chorus:

Oh, what a team you've got.
Oh, what a team you've got.
Oh, you play volleyball,
Oh, how you play volleyball.
You play it in the hall, off the wall,
Please don't fall, you're all so tall.

1st Bridge:

Coaches help to set the pace.
It seems a never-ending race
To try to get an edge on other teams.
Is it all so much to ask
For us to rise up to this task?
It's just a measure of our hopes and dreams, what does it mean?

2nd Verse:

Fee Fee moves just like a cat.
She's lithe and graceful,
Faster than a gnat,
She's never flat.
Marissa serves a cannon blast,
She scores at will
And makes it last all game,
She brings us fame.

Chorus:

2nd Bridge:

You give your all to play this game,
The smiles and laughs are worth the pain,
Moms and Dads can never really know.
All the work goes into it to build a team and make it fit,
Sacrifice is all part of the show,
And you should know.

3rd Verse:

Kylie plays with all her might.
Dives for the ball,
She's such a sight to see.
Don't hurt your knee.
Lyssa sets the ball up high.
Hitters charge and
Let it fly and then
We win again.

Chorus:

3rd Bridge:

You've taken planes and trains and cars
To play this sport – makes you a star,
The world may never ever really see.
But all the work you give this game
Will surely help make you a name,
It all comes down to what you want to be,
Nothing comes free.

Chorus:

Chorus, repeat and fade.

NOTES: "What A Team You've Got" was written to the tune of Plain White T's number 1 hit song, "Hey There, Delilah." I wrote it for my daughter Marissa's high school volleyball team when she was a senior in high school. She was a 4-year starter and letter winner, and team captain. My wife, Aprile, served as the volleyball team's booster club president for several of those years. I performed this song with the father of one of the kids on the team. He played guitar while I sang at the team's awards banquet. I was really blown away when the girls held cell phones aloft recording me while I sang the song to them, so I think they liked it. We got a nice round of applause and a lot of surprised people. Few people knew that I write music and lyrics. But Marissa's master's degree in publishing may change all that. It was fun doing this song for the kids, and Marissa was proud. She also won the top awards for the team, which finished second in a very competitive district.

I wrote this song in October 2008 while driving home from a volleyball match in Dallas, Pa. In a gym packed to the rafters, my daughter's team won over their cross-town rival. The song by Plain White T's came on the radio, and these words to that music came into my head immediately. I drove straight to a local restaurant to pick up my other daughter, Chelsea, a varsity tennis player for the same high school, who was working at the restaurant. While I waited for her I borrowed a pen and wrote the above lyrics on a hoagie wrapper. The song required minimal refinement after I wrote it. It is added to this collection of lyrics because the song contains some nicely-turned phrases capturing adolescent hopes and dreams in sports. This one is for my daughter, Marissa, and for the Crestwood High School volleyball team. May you both always keep on winning.

CHELSEA

She woke up this morning
And told me her dream.
Distorted images
In a world that only seems.

Devoid of connection
Denoting an uncertain past,
A false resurrection,
A promise that won't last.

Her journey has been rocky
On a jagged, slippery shore.
She wrestles with the world
In a tiny, private war.

She longs to break free,
Wants to start anew.
There are those who would help her,
But she fears her debut.

She's a fighter that's certain,
Though her conflict is within.
She doesn't seem to learn
There are battles she can't win.

Someday she will see
That it was all a game
Where the clever survive
And the rest are all the same.

Someday she will know
That her anger was misplaced.
She will change it into kindness.
She will finally find some grace.

Today that time seems distant,
A future yet to come.
But it's one that can be written,
If she only learns to love.

Each day something is given,
And something's taken away.
She'll make the most of living,
    Doing her best every day.

And when all her yesterdays
Are piled high in a penny jar,
Maybe then she'll be happy.
She will have come so far.

NOTES: I wrote this poem for our lovely daughter, Chelsea, on the morning of 9-2-12. Like her twin sister, Marissa, Chelsea is a Thursday's Child with far to go. But aren't we all? "Marissa" appears in Chapter 4. Our beautiful girls are fraternal twins. My wife and I are blessed.

THE CAT

I gave the cat a cup of coffee.
Into traffic she did run.
The cat was no longer interested
In having any fun.

I gave the cat some coffee
To see what she would do.
She ran to a construction site,
And then her lives were few.

Yesterday I gave the cat two cups of coffee
Because I was in a good mood.
She climbed the walls and clawed at some balls,
Then she got stuck in the laundry chute.

Today I gave the cat another cup of coffee.
This time she drank it black.
She rolled on the floor, then she ran out the door,
And I hope she doesn't come back.

Later that night the cat came back.
She brought me a mouse and a bird.
She peed in the sink, and I'd swear she winked,
As I yelled a few choice words.

I know when I'm licked,
The cat's here to stay.
Now she goes in the litter.
There's no other way.

NOTES: This would not be the first time I wrote about a cat. I wrote a set of limericks about cats for a newspaper once. The New Yorker magazine ran a satirical article in 1937 titled "Our Enemy The Cat," which suggested that cats use their human owners to suit their own ends, and most people never realize it. I'm here to tell you I realize it. My wife is a cat lover, and while I'm a dog lover I grudgingly admit to liking the cats also.

So make no mistake, the ideas expressed in "The Cat" are purely fictional for humorous effect, and no animals, living or imaginary, were injured in the telling of it, nor did they get any coffee. Pictured is our cat, Mikey, who was as much like a dog as a he was a cat. Incredibly athletic, he could leap from the floor to the top of the refrigerator in a standing high jump, 6 feet plus. Mice were child's play. His best sport? Ping pong.

My wife is a cat lover, I'm a dog lover. She's had cats since the age of 2. While we've been together we have had 7 cats and 2 dogs, so what does that tell you? If you read a particular comic strip or watch a certain cartoon you might believe 'dogs drool and cats rule.' But whether you describe yourself as a cat lover or a dog lover, the next time you consider bringing a furry friend into your home, please stop by your local SPCA to adopt one of their dogs or cats. I've been affiliated with the SPCA for nearly 30 years, and with few exceptions all of our pets have come from the SPCA. Be they canine or feline, these gentle and loving beings are without a home through no fault of their own. If you are of a mind to adopt, please visit your local SPCA first.

DELECTABLE YOU

You smile your smile,
Your voice floats like a feather.
I can tell all the while
You speak of the weather.

Your sweet baby blues,
They just make me feel,
Quite tame and subdued --
My heart you will steal.

Your honey-colored hair
Is wrapped in a pony.
You make me believe
That sometimes I'm phony.

Your movements are free
Though statuesque you stand.
You're looking at me
And I melt in your hand.

Your laughter is soft.
You keep to yourself.
My eyes drift aloft,
And my mind's on the shelf.

You're kind and content
And inside you're strong.
I lie in lament
And write silly songs.

You spellbind many
With enchantments so true.
You're a confection of plenty,
Dear delectable you.

I guess all in all
You're a two-straw shake,
And you're made of the stuff
That Ma used to bake.

NOTES: I wrote "Delectable You" in the summer of 1979, and I have to believe I had my future wife, Aprile, in the back of my mind. We had just met and she made me a batch of chocolate chip cookies that would put Mrs. Fields out of business. But generally there was no particular woman who was the inspiration for this poem. It was largely word play and sense impressions. OK, it's about Aprile, but she has brown eyes and the character has blue. This prompted a discussion and I had to tell her quite simply that the word "blue" creates considerably more rhyming possibilities than the word "brown." Our exchange reminded me of an old saying in literary circles as an admonition to anyone who would write a sonnet or a love song. It goes something like this: "Blue eyes say 'Love me or I'll die.' Brown eyes say 'Love me or I'll kill you.' The sun rose and set in her eyes."

I KNOW THAT YOU LOVED ME

1st Verse:

It must have been hard for you,
Words could not say.
You gave birth to a baby
On a cold November day.
There was no bouquet of roses
In a room dark and gray.
But the hardest part of all
Was to give your baby away.

2nd Verse:

You were just sixteen,
Not a woman, more a child.
You had your life ahead of you.
I wonder if you smiled,
Knowing you were doing
What was best for your boy,
Second-guessing every minute
And crying tears of joy.

Chorus:

I know that you loved me
By the choices that you made.
I know you were lonely,
I know you were afraid.

I hope and pray you saw
All the love on my face.
And you held me for a moment
In a peaceful warm embrace.

3rd Verse:

I was the son
That you just didn't plan.
I would just like to know
Did you get to hold my hand?
I know, my loved one,
You had help from above.
'Cause the gift that you gave me
Was the most precious form of love.

Chorus:

I know that you loved me
By the choices that you made
I know you were lonely,
I know you were afraid.

I hope and pray you saw
All the love on my face.
And you held me for a moment
In a peaceful warm embrace.

Bridge:

Time can be healing,
Time draws us apart.
It can magnify your feelings,
Or melt and change your heart.

For the longest time I thought
You did not want me at all.
It left me feeling lonely,
It left me feeling small.

But now I understand
My take on it was wrong.
That's why I'd like to say 'I love you,'
That's why I wrote this song.

Chorus:

I know that you loved me
By the choices that you made.
I know you were lonely,
I know you were afraid.

I hope and pray you saw
All the love on my face.
And you held me for a moment
In a peaceful warm embrace.

3rd Verse:

You are my secret hero,
The mother I never knew.
Your courage gave me life.
I owe my chance to you.
But you must realize
It's a debt I can't repay.
The only thing that's left for me
Is to do my best each day.

Chorus:

I know that you loved me
By the choices that you made.
I know you were lonely,
I know you were afraid.

I hope and pray you saw
All the love on my face.
And you held me for a moment
In a peaceful warm embrace.

Chorus:

Repeat and fade

NOTES: The most personal and subjective of all the songs I've written, "I Know That You Loved Me" is autobiographical from start to finish. I'm adopted, and very proud of it. I'm also very proud of this song structurally and content-wise with the ideas that it renders, and the breadth of love that it represents. It took artistic courage to write this because most poets and songwriters will shy away from anything that defines who they are, preferring instead an objective and distant approach. The only exception might be if there's a great story to tell that could be turned into a song, like this one. This song was cathartic for me in that it made me realize how lucky I am to have been adopted, and also just to be alive and to have a chance at life. I view the creation of this song as an act of God working through me and with me, as with many things that are creative. The lines just came to me one fall afternoon and I had to write them down. Those lines became the first verse, and the chorus. But I knew there was more. A day or two went by and the second and third verses came. Then a day later I wrote the bridge. When I put it all together I thought it was beautiful in its simplicity and in its honesty, and I thanked God for letting me write such a powerful message. Months later I wrote the music to it. I think it's a nice song that could be a hit song because of the life-affirming message it relates, as well as a belief in the boundless reaches of love. The lyrics alone can still bring a tear to my eye. If they move me, I think they might move anyone. "I Know That You Loved Me" is based solely on ideas elicited by my imagination, and on my ability to capture and articulate those ideas in written form. I have never met my birth mother, and out of love, honor and respect for my Mom and Dad, whose very memory I cherish, I probably never will. But I want her to know that I am grateful for her love and for her courage. To paraphrase the title of my favorite movie, it's been a wonderful life. And like any great story, there's much more to come.

CHAPTER 4
ALL MY TOMORROWS

AT EASE!

Did the general betray us,
While he tried to evade us,
Or was it just some WAC's ambition?
In the engine of his soul,
Where the colors bend and roll,
Did she turn the key to his ignition?

He's a military man,
All in and true blue.
Stars and stripes,
And he's pointing at you.

Got a chest full of medals,
For the gauntlet fit.
He was born to command
He ain't diggin' no pit.

She's a military woman,
One of the few.
She's ripe at the base,
With chevrons brand new.

Got her own kind of steel,
She can play with the boys.
With legs that won't quit,
Might become someone's toy.

It started with a run,
All he wanted was some fun,
And maybe a pleasant diversion.
But it ended with a bomb,
All he wants is some calm,
And to sink into a private conversion.

You can't fault the man,
He did his job as best he can,
Then he had her when he thought no one was looking.
Was no cyber affair,
She was up in his hair,
He never really knew what she was cooking.

Then another chick got into the fray,
His girl told her to keep the hell away.
Maybe it was mistaken identity?
But his lady got it wrong,
Saw a threat where there was none.
Now they all face double indemnity.

Chorus:

Everybody say 'At ease!'
Everybody just do as you please.
Everybody has a prisoner to seize.
But when you wear the uniform,
You don't get to choose the door,
This is how we run a war.
At Ease!

Repeat Chorus:

She's a player and a pusher,
And a pawn in a game.
But she followed his orders.
She never wanted this fame.

She wanted to be something
That was big in his command.
But a role like this
Was not what she had planned.

Now a good soldier is gone from the stage.
She's left burning in a tempest of rage.
She showed him the spark and he lit the fire.
She lays in a bed with the ashes of desire.

A collateral bitch in a game at the base,
Watch how fast she does about-face.
Meanwhile he still stands at attention,
Holding a bag full of good intentions.

Politics as usual on Capitol Hill,
Four stars bows to the public will.
Clouds of war have lifted from the field.
Sword from the scabbard no longer will he wield.

Chorus:

Everybody say 'At ease!'
Everybody just do as you please.
Everybody has a prisoner to seize.
But when you wear the uniform
You don't get to choose the door.
This is how we run a war.
At ease!

Bridge:

Jill and Paula,
Let me hear you holla,
Go baby!

(Female Vocals)

Two weeks I lived on them messed up C-rations
'Cause you said my khakis were no longer in fashion.
I drove your jeep C-J through a stone wall
When you said your little soldier wouldn't answer the call.

That ain't how we roll.
You gonna learn how to play.
You wanna tap some of this.
You gonna do as I say.

I'm an army of one,
And a fleet times three.
You can't stop this advance
When I come at reveille.

So pay me, don't play me.
If you knew what I know,
On your knees and salute,
Some respect you will show.

(Female vocal, continued, slowly, sweetly)

When you showed me your grenade,
As we toured the promenade,
I was not at all afraid
Because I'd been there before.

Since you're out of ammunition
We can end this demolition.
That ain't no contradiction,
And I won't clean up the floor.

(Female Vocals) Chorus:

(Male Vocals)

Better step lightly into that good night.
There's no telling when your mind takes flight.
In this man's army!

What you got, son?
You don't need to cut and run.
This is how we have some fun,
In this man's army!

Listen up, now we won,
You don't always need a gun,
This is how we get it done,
In this man's army!

Take a walk around,
You can always hear the sound.
You're not lost when you're found,
In this man's army!

Dogs of war are barkin',
In their Jeeps they be parkin',
'Cause some fun they be sparkin'
In this man's Army!

You can put the chopper down
For the troops on the ground.
The chicks ain't comin' round,
In this man's army!

Chorus: (Male and Female Vocals in unison, repeat and close)

© 2012, Michael A. Incitti

NOTES: I wrote this poem/rap song on 11-13-12, 9:13 a.m. to 10:10 a.m. (part 1, male vocals), and 11-14-12, 9 a.m. to 9:15 a.m. (part 2, female vocals), and 11:50 to noon (encore with chorus). The title of this song began as Current Events, but that conveys little of the song contents, so I changed it to "At Ease" in keeping with the overall military theme. Once I had the title I could edit further and refine the chorus. A second revision on 11-15 eliminated small redundancies and non-essential words or syllables to better align rhythm and meter. This rap song is based on real events in the news involving General David Petraeus, a 4-star general and the elite military man of his generation, and Paula Broadwell, a former Army reservist and Petraeus' biographer. The general was director of the C.I.A. at the time he had an affair with his biographer, and he allegedly leaked classified information to her that breached national security. On a broad scale it gave new meaning to the phrase "pillow talk." The reference to 'Jill" in the song is Jill Kelley, identified in news reports as a friend of the general. She said she received threatening emails that were traced to Miss Broadwell. The FBI got involved and indictments soon followed. The irony is that if Paula hadn't become jealous and threatened Jill, odds are no one would have ever known of the general's dalliance. These events are a movie waiting to happen. Like "A Better Way" and "Sum Of Your Parts," "At Ease" resulted in an interesting rap song. I can see Bruno Mars and his posse running with this one. The song began with the phrase "Did General Petraeus really betray us?" and I ran with that theme. But my good friend and professional 4-star guitarist Greg Rai, of Long Island, N.Y., suggested I take out the general's name so the song could last longer because of the broader story it depicts. I changed the beginning without losing rhythm or rhyme.

I FORGOT TO SAY GOODBYE

I forgot to say goodbye.
I forgot to say goodbye.
And I don't mind,
It's so hard to say,
I'd rather not try.
I can't look your way.
No, no I'll never stray.

I forgot to say how much.
I forgot to say how much
You mean to me.
You're all that I know.
I'll leave if you want.
There's nowhere to go.
No, no don't close the door.

Chorus:

I tried to make you see
That I love you,
There's nobody else.
No one can compare,
The light in your eyes,
The warmth of your smile, for me.

I just want to say hello.
I just want to say hello,
And start again.
It's easy to do,
If both of us try,
You'll give me a clue.
Yes, yes we'll start anew.

I just want to say, you're mine.
I just want to say, you're mine,
You always were.
Right from the start
I knew in one look
That you held my heart.
We'll never be apart.

Chorus:

Repeat, and fade…..

NOTES: This is another rare song for me in which the music preceded the lyrics. It's written in E flat with several minor chords. I wrote the music late in 2011, and then I refined it by mid-2012. The lyrics finally came to me on 1-10-13 in one writing session starting at 10:30 p.m. and ending on 1-11-13 at 1 a.m. With a goal of simplicity, only one word has 3 syllables. The syllables and the tempo fit, but it took me a couple of days of playing it to recognize its structural integrity. It's very clean with a nice instrumental flourish at the end.

ALL MY TOMORROWS

1st Verse:

If I could arrange maybe
All my tomorrows
I'd still want you here by my side.
But just like the wind you will change
And I won't see you go.
But I still want you to know I love you so.

Instrumental Bridge

2nd Verse:

If I had one wish about
All my tomorrows
I'd spend every second with you.
Our time goes too fast when we grieve.
I cannot let you go.
Yes, I still want you to know I love you so.

Instrumental Bridge

Repeat Instrumental Intro.

3rd Verse:

The stars up above tell me
All my tomorrows
Will still keep me there by your side.
And just like the sun I will shine.
My love will never go.
And I still want you to know I love you so.

Instrumental Bridge

Close:

Too many people spinning round in my head.
Too many voices remind me what I read.
Too many miles now to go before I sleep.
Too many dreams to sow before I reap.

Instrumental Bridge

Instrumental Close

NOTES: This song also began with the music alone in the key of C. I dedicated this song to our friends Greg Rai and his wife, Lorna, of Long Island, N.Y. Greg and I have been friends since our days at Bloomsburg and at Temple, now 38 years. I wrote the music on 11-27-12 and 2-11-13, months apart. Around the time I finished the music, the lyrics came to me on Feb. 11-13, 2013. I added a lyrical bridge and an instrumental close on July 6, 2013. This is one of my structural favorites. It represents solid construction of music and lyrics for a simple song that conveys everlasting love and devotion in just over three minutes.

I RIDE THIS TRAIN

1st Verse:

I ride this train from day to day.
Nobody knows what I have to say.
I ride this track of endless miles
Searching the faces for a trace of a smile.

I ride this train to places unknown.
Sometimes I wonder if my spirit has flown.
Buildings and scenery pass in a blur.
You forget where you're from, you forget who you were.

I ride this train to a gig up town.
Over the bridge, cab ride brings me down.
Driver turns with an icy stare.
I reach in my pocket and pay the fare.

Working the bars and the clubs and the dives
Sometimes you feel only half-alive.
Last few dates we didn't get paid.
Pack up the gear and back on the train.

Chorus:

But when I play my guitar the sound takes me far.
Breaks me out of my shell, and the audience can tell.
I'm the leader of the band, driving rhythm in my hands.
All the notes ride in my brain on this lonely, cross-town train.

2nd Verse:

The night people come, drinks firmly in hand.
Cigarettes slowly burn, smoke circles the band.
We play our set to a loud ovation.
They don't know our name, lost in their libation.

We work the crowd with songs they know.
R&B, funk and a little bit of soul.
Tonight the club is ours -- they shout their requests.
Our set ends at three, but we still don't get no rest.

Club owner says there's a gig up the street.
Said the place is owned by his brother.
I said pay us now or we might bring the heat.
He paid us for one, but said forget about the other.

Back on the train collecting the moments,
We've come so far, with far to go.
This endless journey on a solitary track
Makes me long for a quiet studio.

Chorus:

Bridge:

Two blondes in white shirts with late-summer tans
Are lifted by their boyfriends and thrust toward the band.
They both caught my eye, but one looked right through me.
I knew what she wanted; she could not confuse me.

Told her I'd call next time I passed through,
But she knew that's a card I would never play.
The timing was wrong like notes to a song
With a rhythm you just can't betray.

Chorus:

Repeat chorus and fade

© 2012, 2013, Michael A. Incitti

NOTES: This was another song written as a tribute to my good friend and fellow musician Greg Rai, a guitarist, arranger, and composer. It stemmed from a conversation in which he told me about his band's ongoing challenges to get gigs in a tough market. The first 7 lines were written in November 2012, and the rest of the poem was written on 3-5, 3-7 and 3-8-13. Greg, a.k.a. "G," or "Gibbs," and I have always encouraged each other, and provided feedback and a sounding board for our respective musical and literary pursuits. Through the decades, we still believe.

LOST AND FOUND

1st Verse:

You were lost, then found.
Both feet off the ground.
And then there you were in the rain.
It poured all around
The streets of the town.
With nowhere to run
And nowhere to hide
Seeking shelter from the storm outside.
A night so dark and cold,
There's no hand to hold.

Chorus:

I will find you, just
Look behind you right now.
Rain upon your face,
Tears won't leave a trace now.
Words don't say enough, my love.
Cards won't let me bluff, my love.
But still you ran away.
You have no time to play.
I only want to say,
I love you so much it makes me cry.
Without you I'll die.

Minor Bridge:

Please believe in me.
You don't have to see
My love for you is here
In the touch of my hand.

1st Bridge:

How sad when we're apart.
How glad you make my heart.
How fast the sands of time.
Our love had strength to climb.
Our love had wings to fly.

2nd Verse:

You were lost, then found
Both feet off the ground.
Hoping only to end all the pain.
From the life you had known.
Your heart now has flown.
Your face everywhere,
I need you with me,
Seeking shelter from a stormy sea.
A night so dark and cold,
Here's my hand to hold.

Chorus:

2nd Bridge:

Now she's safe in my arms.
I'll know all of her charms.
Her feet on the ground.
To my heart she is bound.
She was lost now she's found.

Instrumental Close:

© 2012, 2013, Michael A. Incitti

NOTES: The music came first with this song in the key of C, so the task was to put words to the music. My goal was tell a story with the utmost simplicity. No word exceeds two syllables, with a clean metric and rhythm. It has some nice melodic movement with the music building to a climax. This might be a case where the music is better than the lyrics. I wrote the music in mid-September 2012, with lyrics to follow a few months later on Nov. 18, 19 and 20. I like this song, and not just because I wrote it. If you find yourself humming your song even while you work outside in your garden then either you have something or you need to get away from it.

MARISSA

Children get older.
Winters get colder.
I just want to hold her.
But my little girl has grown.

There's so much I want to say.
Sometimes the past gets in the way.
I long for another day
To teach her what I know.

Her life was a surprise.
She has her mother's eyes.
She sees through my disguise.
Where did the years all go?

She stands strong on her own two feet,
Finds her way through cold or heat
She marches softly to her own beat.
Harvests her dreams to reap and sow.

I stand in awe of the things she's done,
Amazed by the woman my daughter's become.
The struggles she's fought, the battles she's won,
And none of it was done for show.

Hair of gold and earth eyes so deep,
Her memories await, treasures to keep.
Sometimes in silence I will weep,
For my little girl has grown.

The little girl that I once knew,
Became a beauty in days too few.
With heart and soul and mind so true,
Maybe it's time for me to go.

Children get older.
Winters get colder.
I just want to hold her.
But my little girl has grown.

© 2013, Michael A. Incitti

NOTES: I wrote this on 1-24-13, from 1 to 2 p.m. through my cell phone in the car while driving home from Millersville after taking my daughter Marissa back to college. I would pull into a rest area and call my office phone each time a stanza came to me -- 9 calls in 20-30 second intervals to write 7 stanzas – and dictate it to voicemail. Next morning I reversed the order of the last two stanzas, and repeated the first to end the song with an even 8. This lyric poem is for our darling daughter, Marissa, my little publisher, and fraternal twin sister of Chelsea.

Angels, Ceramic and Otherwise: *Not long after I was born a neighbor brought me a gift. An art teacher and painter, her name was Emily and she had made me two ceramic angels. One had light brown hair, almost golden, and the other had dark brown hair. These intricately-painted little sculptures were about the size of an adult hand. They were in the form of a cherubic angel's head with wings. My mother hung them on the wall in the little room that was my bedroom. As an infant I had difficulty sleeping. Mom told me the angels were there to watch over me and to protect me as I slept. All of my life - from childhood through adolescence and then adulthood when I came home to visit -- those angels hung on the wall overlooking the bed in that little room. A year after my wife gave birth to our twin daughters, one with light brown hair, the other with dark brown hair, we went to visit my Mom and Dad. As we brought the girls to the little room for a nap, I noticed the angels were gone. Mom was always giving things to the church for charity drives, so I thought that's where the angels went, which was a good place for them. Age and time had left my mother with a slight touch of dementia, and she could not recall what she did with the angels, or when they left the little room. I gave my Mom a hug and a kiss and said "That's OK Mom, the angels did their job." Later that night, as my wife and I looked in on our infant girls, it occurred to me that I still had my two angels after all. We watched them for a few moments as they slept soundly in that little room. And I knew then as their father that it was now my turn to return the favor that Emily and the ceramic angels had given me so long ago.*

DAY IN THE SUN

I had my day in the sun.
I left no work undone.
I waged many battles to be won.
Thinking back now, it wasn't all fun.
Because sometimes they booed and they jeered.
And they questioned my choice of career.
They doubted my skill at hurling this sphere.
But there were days on the mound when I had no peer.

My days in the sun they were few.
But I felt so alive and so new.
Throwing ninety-five miles per hour on cue –
The smell of the grass, the warm summer dew.
Now I play baseball here in my mind.
I miss my old teammates, the contracts I signed.
Looking back now I knew nothing better I'd find.
But the seasons with speed, they sure did unwind.

My day in the sun went too fast.
My all-star seasons flew past.
World Series pitchers don't last,
Just a bit player in the MLB cast.
That was the time of my life.
Now I've got a great family and wife.
Sometimes not playing baseball cuts like a knife.
But I'd do it again in a moment despite all the strife.

My day in the sun now seems brief.
What I miss most is the chance to compete.
The money and cars, those you can keep.
Since I gave it my all there is no defeat.
If I could go back tomorrow and play,
If only for just one more blessed day,
I would stand proudly on that mound of clay,
And pitch the baseball again until the sun fades away.

NOTES: This poem was inspired by a brief conversation with retired MLB pitcher, Andy Ashby, who had married a woman from Northeast Pa. I was the referee for a basketball game in which he was coaching his daughters. We talked under the basket after the game. Next day in my office the first few lines came to me, and the rest followed.

BARELY THERE

1st Verse:

Her voice is so small.
You can hardly hear her at all.
Her words disperse in the air,
Like a hummingbird, here and there.
You still can't hear what she said.
Her words never reach your head.
A look in her eyes says she knows.
Her good intentions will someday show.

Chorus:

She is barely there.
Her voice is lighter than air.
She's suspended in time,
Waving goodbye,
Without a destination or a care.

She is barely there.
Her energy fades on a dare.
She's frozen in flight,
Turn out the light,
Without a moment to spare.

2nd Verse:

Sweep it under the seat,
Like all the people you meet.
It's never the same,
But they're not to blame.
Look away and you're gone.
Steal the night from the dawn.
When will you rise and fly away?
When will you have something to say?

Chorus:

Bridge:

She needs to be aware
That her talent is rare.
Nine out of ten miss the point.
The glitter on her cheeks
Makes you want to take a peek.
She walks in and lights up the joint.

Chorus:

Repeat and fade

NOTES:I wrote this on Jan. 14, 2014, at the International Airport in Newark, N.J. I had a two-hour layover between business flights so I did what I like to do: observe and people-watch and use my imagination. The title for the song came to me a few weeks before, but I had no words, just a vague idea. Then a few images at the airport caught my eye and fragments of conversations caught my ear, and suddenly I had 8 lines and a partial chorus. The rest of the poem was fleshed out a month later.

THE KING

Elvis was the king,
There's no questioning that.
The world was his kitchen
Most everywhere he sat.

Took the biggest bite
From the rock and roll pie.
Owned the record charts
Until the day he died.

If you go to Memphis
You will notice him still.
He's in the hearts of all,
A legend time can't kill.

All who try are measured
By the stars who went before.
But none shone bright as Elvis,
Still honored by troubadours.

So you come to Nashville
With your heart on your sleeve.
Your head is in the clouds
With a pocket full of dreams.

You have a few connections
To help you on your way.
But when you show them your work
They don't know what to say.

You wander to a bar,
Guitar slung on your back.
Guy comes up to you, says
Help us lay down a track.

The room is quiet, eyes intent,
You begin to play and sing.
There's talk in the booth – ain't it the truth --
You may be the next big thing.

Next thing you know you're on the card at the Opry.
Some big names brush past you backstage.
You can't hide your jitters – all that glows doesn't glitter –
But when your turn comes your music is the rage.

After the show you sign a deal
And soon you're out on the road.
But the songs won't come, and the crowds won't hum.
You find you can't carry the load.

Back on the streets of Memphis, Tennessee,
You pray for a break – you'll sing for free.
'Just give me a place to play my songs,
I don't care about the dream.'

The streets are cold as the rain starts to pour.
You look up and follow the light.
A sign above a door says enter this way.
You take two steps to your right.

The door opens to a hall where a service just begins.
All is quiet then the choir starts to sing.
You fall into the pew, the music washes over you.
Your spirit soars as keyboard and voices ring.

After a song the piano player looks at you
With an eye that says she knows.
She asks you to join and you're happy to oblige.
You step into the footlights' glow.

Now Brenda plays piano,
Every Friday night at eight.
She's got no time for posers.
She's got no time for hate.

Says 'Can you sing some gospel, child?
'Lift your voice up to the sky.
'Sing it loud and sing it strong,
'Make the angels cry.'

Just then a voice whispers in your ear,
'If you sing for God then everyone will hear.
'Do it for yourself and do it for Him,
'Before the light of your talent dims.'

You sing with your heart
And you sing with your soul.
You give it all you've got,
And the choir is on a roll.

Brenda says she likes you with the choir,
But she knows you're a solo onstage.
'If you've got the fire, you'll keep going higher,
'But your heart is always your gauge.'

You tell her you'll give it all you've got
For another chance to share your voice.
There's no in-between, you say what you mean,
Your actions follow your choice.

As the crowd dispersed someone wondered aloud,
Who was that fellow in the back of the hall?
If I didn't know better I'd say it was the king.
Come back to answer a blues singer's call.

NOTES: There are few artists past or present who can lay claim to not only influencing entire generations of artists and fans, but of shaping the very course of a seminal and pervasive genre of music, rock and roll. In many ways, Elvis Presley stands without peer in professional music, and he continues to inspire song content and musical styles long after he passed in 1977 at age 42. This tribute came in separate parts with the first three stanzas about Elvis in the fall of 2012. The two stanzas with Brenda, the pianist, were written in spring 2013. The inspiration for her is an actual pianist, piano prodigy Brenda Nighbert from Northeast, Pa. She and I had a duo act. I would sing songs from musicals and the great American songbook. Opry is a reference to the Grand Ole Opry house in Nashville. Another artist in the background of this tribute includes one of my favorites, singer/songwriter and guitarist Harry Chapin, who also died far too young at age 38 in 1981.

ONCE WHEN WE WERE YOUNG

It happened long ago
But I remember it still.
The places we went,
The time we spent,
We made that old Buick go.

It happened in the spring
Before semester's end.
We parked at a lake,
Drank wine and ate cake,
While we watched the flowers grow.

It happened in the summer.
I saw you by a pool.
We talked until midnight,
And hid beneath the moonlight
On the green before a fire's glow.

It happened in the fall.
We began to drift apart.
The phone calls we missed,
The passionless kiss,
Foretold what we both came to know.

It happened in the winter.
Our love came to an end.
We walked in silence through an empty park.
We tried to find answers, but then it got dark.
Snow fell through the lamplight to the frozen ground below.

Once when we were young
We had the time of our lives.
We cherished the best, forgot the rest,
And sometimes we would just drive.

It's human nature to think about
The girl you leave behind.
As we travel on life's journey
We never know what we may find.

I wish you peace and happiness.
I hope your days don't fly too fast.
I hope you remember the time we spent,
And I hope you found love that lasts.

NOTES: Written in May 2013, this lyric poem is a collection of memories from old girlfriends, embellished for literary effect. The title and the first two lines just came to me while I was walking up the stairs in the house late in the evening. I don't know where the lines came from, but I had to write them down. Once I wrote them the rest followed. I knew I had something so I went back to my desk next to the piano and wrote from 10:30 p.m. to midnight and beyond on 5-7-13. While driving home in the rain after a baseball game on the afternoon of 5-8-13, I thought about what I wrote and then a few other ideas came to mind. These were added and others removed. As with "Still Water," written a few days before, this poem is somewhat experiential, but with imagination and extrapolation. Content-wise this work is a simple chronological progression moving from season to season. It is inspired by the works of some of my favorite composers, structurally Stevie Wonder, with color and tone influenced by Paul Simon. I wrote "Once When We Were Young" and "Still Water," in Chapter 8, in a couple of days. When both arrived it was a relief because I hadn't written anything in months. I feared my Muse had left me. But she came back.

THE MUSE

Clarity finds you
On a cold December day.
All the fields are fallow,
Sound asleep in their way.

Taxi brings you home,
You're staring into space.
Your breath on the window
Hides the lines on your face.

You stepped off of one flight
Only to begin another.
Kettle starts to boil,
Thoughts the cold cannot smother.

The winter snow falls outside,
Silent and soft as cotton.
It tosses your dreams in the swirling wind
Arousing images long forgotten.

Ghostlike she rises through the wintry haze,
A strange and sullen apparition.
Is she here to remind you of what you once knew?
Or is she the face of your superstition?

You can never know the mystery
Of the human heart.
You cannot unravel history
Before it's meant to start.

This perpetual debutante,
Whose intentions lie on the shelf,
Demands a dour perfection
She would not ask of herself.

Her sources are many
Through vast time and space.
She yields her visions
When you're in the right place.

Who is this muse?
She comes and goes as she pleases.
A girl you once knew
Whose laughter now teases?

Darkness has fallen,
The constellations align.
A flickering symmetry
Lights the night sky.

You cannot join them
In this new dance.
The muse cast her spell,
But she withdrew the chance.

Imperfection drives beauty,
Creates the allure.
Disconnection sparks duty,
You can taste it for sure.

Winter winds whip the snow.
The moon waxes and wanes.
Flakes scatter like diamonds
Against your windowpane.

In a flash she's gone.
Will she come another day?
In her game you're a pawn,
And the taxi pulls away.

NOTES: "The Muse" tries to capture the elusiveness of that spark of inspiration -- the muse who can be here now and then is gone in a mercurial moment. It was written in four waves. The 12th stanza was written in September 2012 as part of a collection of ideas and sense impressions. The first two stanzas were written in early December. I kept coming back to them, but nothing followed. Then I focused on those lines late at night on 1-27-13. The next morning, I just started writing and the remaining 11 stanzas came out almost verbatim. The dreamlike quality is an attempt to reflect the mystery of the creative state, and the ephemeral, oblique nature of the muse herself. The movement depicted from outside to inside represents the process of gathering external stimuli and arranging it internally to meet the demands of a subject. I've enjoyed Greek and Roman mythology from the time I was in junior high. The Muses are 9 goddesses who are the daughters of Zeus and Mnemosyne. Calliope and Erato are the muses of poetry, and Euterpe presides over music.

CHAPTER 5
PORTRAITS OF THE DAY

A CHILD OF WAR

Intro.

A frightened child runs through smoke-filled streets.
So many sad and lonely faces he meets.
Warplanes above eclipse a cloudless sky
With broken wings and things that no longer fly.
The ground would shake, his head would ache 'til he cried.

1st Verse:

No one is coming to stop the noise.
The infantry lands and they move just like toys.
I can't see tomorrow because I'm afraid for today.
People's cries are silenced by
The rockets that rip through the sky.
Buildings would fall, bodies would crawl, but they can't get away.

Instrumental Bridge

Chorus:

Hi, how are you, do you really know my name?
I was once like you, all the faces were the same.
Once I could see only what was close at hand,
Until my eyes were opened by the hunger in this land.
So few lift a finger, and fewer understand.
But no one is to blame.

Bridge:

A world away a child would play
With a helicopter toy.
He'd lower the chain, save them from the rain,
The plastic soldiers of a boy.
Two children worlds apart,
One's reality would break the other's heart.
While one plays in a box of sand,
The other hides from an unseen hand.

2nd Verse:

Where are the flowers that once grew so sweet?
Are they dead and gone far beneath my feet?
Oh, the night is so cold, it gives orders I just can't obey.
What's happened to the home I once knew?
Has it fallen and crumbled from view?
My parents are gone, my friends have moved on, and I know I can't stay.

Instrumental Bridge

Chorus:

Hi, how are you, do you really know my name?
Any avenue, all the faces were the same.
Once I could see only what was close at hand,
Until my eyes were opened by the hunger in this land.
So few lift a finger, and fewer understand.
But no one is to blame. No one is to blame.

Repeat Intro.

A frightened child runs through smoke-filled streets.
So many sad and lonely faces he meets.
Warplanes above eclipse a cloudless sky
With broken wings and things that no longer fly.
The ground would shake, his head would ache 'til he cried.

Instrumental Close

NOTES: The music came first for "A Child Of War," but I had no idea for lyrics, or the nature of the song. I had a vague idea that it was an anti-war or protest song. I had written the music for the introduction and the verses on 12-17-12. It sat there. I liked it, but I didn't know how to proceed. Then on 8-30-13 I came up with the chorus and lyrics. I linked the chorus in E flat to the first melody in E minor, which identified the theme of the song. The verses appear in the key of G. Once I had the chorus, and the theme of war from a child's perspective, the verses came in a burst and lined up note by note, with minimal revision needed on the lyrics. I edited, arranged and wrote the musical bridge and close on 9-2-13, Labor Day, working 8 hours. This song came primarily from my desire to write an anti-war song as hostilities increased in Syria. A television news clip of children running amid swirling smoke stuck in my mind. I originally titled the song "A Child of Syria," and I repeated the phrase "A child of Syria, you know that he needs a miracle" where the instrumental bridge goes. But I removed the line so that the song could have a broader application. I also wanted to keep the music alone in the bridge, which builds to intensity then explodes into the chorus. I like this song, both musically and lyrically. I never throw away a scrap of lyrics or a couple of chords I like. This is one of my favorite songs for its thematic consistency, rhyme, meter and overall poetic unity. I consider this one of my best works to date. The flower reference in the second verse is a nod to folk legend Pete Seeger's classic war protest song, "Where Have All the Flowers Gone?" as sung by Peter, Paul and Mary.

Additional Note: The only element this song lacked was a pure lyrical bridge, a middle eight. Around midnight on Jan. 11, 2014, I wrote one. It came to me just before I fell asleep. I was thinking about collectible items I had once owned. I remembered an old Batman lunch box, and an Army Red Cross helicopter that my parents gave me when I was a toddler. It was my only Christmas gift that year as I spent the holiday in a hospital getting my tonsils out. It occurred to me that the ideal bridge for "A Child of War" would be a contrasting view of another child from the other side of the world. The horrors of war and its collateral damage to children are the same in any time period, whether WWII, Vietnam, or the Middle East. The lines came to me immediately, and I added them on 1-11-14. The music for the bridge came on 1-24-14 when I used a slower tempo variation of the introduction for dramatic effect.

BENEFICIAL FRIENDS

1st Verse:

She was a housewife
In an ordinary world.
Two kids and two dogs,
One with hair that curled.

When they were first married
They played it fast and loose.
Until they woke one morning
With their heads in a noose.

They vowed to change their ways,
And then the kids came.
He kept his promise and got a job,
But for her it was still the same.

She kisses him goodbye each day
On their front porch steps.
When he leaves she locks the door,
And she goes where the laptop's kept.

Chorus:

Summer in the shade,
Winter in the park.
The sky is hazy gray,
We're not out on a lark.
Spring in the heathers,
Autumn in the field.
Whatever the weather
She finds a reason to yield.

Bite the pillow,
Arch your back.
Ride that train
On a one-way track.
The trip is short,
But it never ends.
Another day, another face,
Another beneficial friend.

2nd Verse:

She lives for this hour
Before the children arise.
Needs to know she's a looker -
Still attractive to the guys.

She doesn't really know
Just what she's looking for.
But she knows it when she sees it;
She lets her robe fall to the floor.

She tries to stay away
But her lust's in overdrive.
She's drawn to this game
Like a bee to the hive.

She's in over her head
She won't compromise.
All she wants is a friend
Who will listen to her lies.

Chorus:

Bridge:

All she really wanted
Was a little attention.
She just wanted to do
Those things you don't mention.

She was weak in the knees,
He was thick in the throat.
Neither tried to please,
And that was all she wrote.

Hotel room, secluded lot,
She never stopped to think about
What she has or what she's got.
Look at her life in pieces now.
She doesn't know why,
But she sure knows how.

3rd Verse:

She doesn't like to say
That it's casual sex.
Has to satisfy her need,
It's like taming T-Rex.

Says that she's selective
And just a bit curious.
She's never reflective.
It would make him furious.

One day she met someone
Who made her think twice.
Holding hands was all they did.
She thought it was really nice.

You might think she'd see
The error of her ways.
Her book is only half complete --
But cold nights turn to empty days.

Chorus:

She was a housewife
In an ordinary world.
Two kids and two dogs,
One with hair that curled.

NOTES: The title came to me a year before I wrote "Beneficial Friends," but I had no idea how to approach the topic. While waiting in line at a grocery store I overheard fragments of a conversation between two women. It lasted maybe 2 minutes, but the content dealt with the targeted theme and the connection was immediate. I went home and wrote 6 pages of notes longhand on my yellow legal pad on 6-24-13. Then on 6-30-13 just past midnight to 2:16 a.m. I wrote the entire piece. The opening lines would not let me sleep. "She was a housewife in an ordinary world, two kids and two dogs, one with hair that curled." That kept repeating in my mind. I had to know what happened, so I got up and wrote it. This narrative portrait could fit either genre of popular music or country.

HALOGEN QUEEN

Chorus:

Oh yes, the halogen queen
Is out on a midnight ride.
Tires squeal like a cat in moonlight,
Cigarettes by her side.
What does she seek on a cold fall night?
What does she want to be?
Someone to say it'll be all right,
Someone to set her free?

1ˢᵗ Verse:

Her halogen lights they
Would shine like no other,
Turn the night inside out,
She's the one.

Her jeans were always tight,
Sprayed on like her mother's.
There was no room for doubt
She had fun.

1ˢᵗ Minor Bridge:

Long blonde hair to the middle of her back,
Flying in the wind like threads of gold.
A song on the radio about a love shack,
Time stands still, she will never get old.

Chorus:

Oh yes, the halogen queen
Is out on a midnight ride.
Tires squeal like a cat in moonlight.
Cigarettes by her side.
What does she seek on a cold fall night?
What does she want to be?
Someone to say it'll be all right,
Someone to set her free?

2nd Verse:

'Bout half past eleven
She leaves the burger place.
Throws the apron, she won't
Stop to eat.

Her top down on Route One,
It's made for drag racing.
Pops the clutch and trembles
In her seat.

2nd Minor Bridge:

She smiles to herself 'cause the night is her friend.
It's her time to drive her car and clear her mind.
Tomorrow she's in school and that never ends.
Tonight she will ride where the road wants to wind.

Chorus:

Oh yes, the halogen queen
Is out on a midnight ride.
Tires squeal like a cat in moonlight,
Cigarettes by her side.
What does she seek on a cold fall night?
What does she want to be?
Someone to say it'll be all right,
Someone to set her free?

Bridge:

So you think it's time to go,
But you don't know what to say.
Your emotions aren't your own.
It don't matter anyway.

They see you on the street
Trav'ling far from your home.
You can fool the ones you meet,
Long as you know where to roam.

Bridge continued:

She's the kind of girl who attracts attention
Almost everywhere she goes.
She's the type of girl who has no pretension.
There's a lot of things she knows.

Night calls you from your bed.
It keeps you from your dreams.
You can't recall the words they said,
Nothing ever is what it seems.
Nothing ever is what it seems.

3rd Verse:

She's back way past midnight.
The Mustang's engine hums.
Parks her bright red machine,
Shuts it down.

Her mother cut the lights.
She tossed another bum.
While the Halogen Queen
Wears her crown.

3rd Minor Bridge:

She grabs her car keys, kisses Mom goodbye.
Pacific Coast Highway calls her name.
It's time to drive in her cathedral of speed,
Time to get back to that place from where she came.

Chorus:

Oh yes, the halogen queen
Is out on a midnight ride.
Tires squeal like a cat in moonlight,
Cigarettes by her side.
What does she seek on a cold fall night?
What does she want to be?
Someone to say it'll be all right,
Someone to set her free?

4th Minor Bridge:

Headlights cut the night like a half million suns.
She slides it into fifth and overdrive.
She has no destination with a tank full of gas.
Don't know where she's going but she feels alive.

Chorus:

Instrumental Close

NOTES: The music to the chorus came to me in late spring 2013, and it sat there. The music came first with this song. Then the lyrics to the chorus came to me in late summer. On the morning of Nov. 5, 2013, the first 8 lines of the first verse came to me, then that evening I wrote the rest of the song, 3 verses in all with the chorus. I had to flesh out the character to determine who she was, what she drove, where, and why. The narrative wasn't bad as it stood, but it needed a bridge. I looked in my notes and found the bridge, part of which I had written in mid-summer. I was at a gas station and a girl got out of her car from the bay next to me. She wore a bright red halter top, jeans shorts and high heels. I thought, "She must attract a lot of attention." I wrote what became the third 4-line stanza of the bridge and saved it. When the song needed the complete bridge, I built it around that stanza. I used a lot of one-syllable words that appear in short bursts like an engine's pistons. The song isn't based on anything or anyone I know; it's completely from my imagination driven by the melody - pun intended. The main character is a blonde teenager, a California girl who drives a red Mustang. She's the type of girl the Beach Boys used to sing about. The car is her escape. It's also her peace of mind, and her gateway to the world as she drives along the Pacific Coast Highway. She could have been a prom queen, but she marches to her own beat, so she's the "Halogen Queen." The halogen lights are a metaphor for her finding her own way in the world. This song was a forward movement for me in the process of songwriting. I used a disciplined approach to create the music and to sculpt the lyrics to fit a defined meter. By imposing music on the lyrics, the lyrics were tightened and clarified. On 12-15-13 I wrote the 4th minor bridge after 3 full verses. It was better than repeating the first minor bridge, and it brought the song back to its beginning with headlights front and center.

ONCE IS NOT ENOUGH

1st Verse:

I can feel you looking at me
With sexy eyes that do more than see.
Provocation is in the air.
Did no one teach you not to stare?

I really don't mind your inquiring eyes.
Harmless flirtation – no one tells any lies.
That ring on your finger tells me all I need to know.
Can't let my eyes linger, or my desires will show.

Chorus:

You can act in your play
And keep on pretending
I won't stick around
To see your comical ending.

If you're in it for the game
This is one I won't play.
'Cause once is not enough.
I see that look on your face.

2nd Verse:

Honey-brown hair with eyes like a doe,
Devil-may-care with a body that knows.
All your little signals keep running through my brain.
You've got me on the move like a locomotive train.

Your hips have rhythm as you glide across the room.
Your eyes hold my gaze, there's nothing I can do.
The music is drowned by the pounding of my heart.
I got a wife and kids, I don't want a new start.

Bridge:

You know that I want you,
You know I won't taunt you.
This connection comes once in a blue moon.
In your little red dress
There's no need to confess.
Must keep control or I'll leave with you soon.

Instrumental Bridge

Chorus:

3rd Verse:

Alone at the bar as the night winds down,
I see you to my left – smiling eyes above a frown.
You start to walk toward me – oh no, not again.
You hold out your hand – 'Is this your lapel pin?'

Then I remember my pin fell to the floor.
I saw her bend over and it made me want more.
Guess I'm the fool in a game I never played.
Good thing I didn't or my heart she would have slayed.

Chorus:

Repeat and Fade

NOTES: "Once Is Not Enough" was written on 6-19-13, from 7 to 8 a.m. with editing done on 6-20 from 9 to 10 a.m. I woke up with the first four lines in my head, then I sat down with pen in hand and the rest just poured out. I never go to bars or clubs of any type. I don't drink and I never smoked. I run a business, referee high school sports, and I write and perform music. I figure that's enough. Most important, I'm married to a lovely woman, my wife Aprile. This song aims for suspense, and then a twist at the end. Virtually all human action and discourse is based on perceptions and the expectations they create. In the context of man-woman interaction that concept is crystal clear.

SHE'S LEAVING

For everything she was,
For everything she'd be,
He was tired of giving
So that she could be free.

For everything he was,
For everything he's not,
She was tired of living
In the land of 'you ain't got.'

She packed up her things
And she got on a plane.
She went as far west
As she could to stay sane.

He sat and wondered.
Then he laughed 'till he cried.
He'll never know what might have been.
But he was too tired to try.

She has no secrets
From the life she knew before.
She has no regrets.
She just closed another door.

She got pretty slim,
When they ran the gym,
No one worked more hours.
He taught some classes,
And he worked the women's asses.
Each was to him a flower.

The gym soon closed.
It happened while he dozed.
But she had taught a class of her own.
You could hear her bright and early
With a guy whose hair was curly.
Listen closely, you could hear her moan.

Then he drove a truck,
And it helped him turn his luck.
He made money till it fell from his pants.
She was home alone.
She grew tired of the phone.
So she dared to take another chance.

She met another in a bar,
She went too fast, he went too far.
He found her in the parking lot.
She was in the back seat
Opening a new treat,
But in seconds the guy was shot.

She knew who did it, but she wouldn't say.
He bought her ticket; he paid her way.
In return she was quiet as a mouse.
He agreed to let her leave,
The lies he knew she could not weave.
He watched the plane fly over their house.

For everything she was,
For everything she'd be,
He was done with giving
So that she could be free.

For everything he was,
For everything he's not,
She was happy she was leaving
The land of 'you ain't got.'

She packed up her things
And she got on that plane.
She was flying far west
Above an eastbound train.

He bought her silence;
He paid for her flight.
And no one ever asked
What was wrong or what was right.

Now she has a secret
From the life she knew before.
She still has no regrets.
She just opened a new door.

NOTES: "She's Leaving" is somewhat based on an actual story about people who were in the news in Northeast Pennsylvania. I added a significant amount of embellishment and literary license with plot though to make the story more compelling. It might work as a country song. I didn't set out to write about this particular topic, but the first few stanzas came to me and I had to figure out who 'he' and 'she' were and what their story was about. Once I had the beginning the story came quickly. But the meat and potatoes of the story lies with its considerable literary reconstruction. The result is a straight-up, straight-shot poem in simple language without bridges or choruses or instrumentals. It tells a clean narrative that has its own rhythms and keeps driving forward to the close.

LIMITS TO HER LOVE

1st Verse:

I saw her on the corner
Waiting near the shop.
I asked her to come to me.
She said the rain won't stop.

I said that's fine for you
Because that's how you are.
You refuse to stay the course.
You refuse to fight for par.

Chorus:

There are limits to her love
She will always second-guess.
There are boundaries she won't cross.
There are thoughts she will suppress.

There are limits to her love.
There are lines of demarcation.
There are fragments of her heart
In pieces on the pavement.

2nd Verse:

She seemed so deferential.
Calm and quiet without a care.
What I thought was potential
Became a solar flare.

When I put it all together
It just did not make sense.
To the mean she's a regression,
And she lacks all confidence.

Chorus:

Bridge:

To you it's all the same.
Call me vile,
Call me vain.
There are no other names
For you to speak.

But I did it all for you.
All the while
Staying true.
My color's always blue.
It's you I seek.

3rd Verse:

She said the rain is coming
And she's getting very wet.
I said I'd heard that line before.
Her words are like a bayonet.

I lived with her oppression.
There are no ghosts and goblins.
She is unaware of her indiscretion.
And now the rain is not my problem.

Chorus:

4th Verse

Yesterday I saw her on the corner.
She was waiting near that very same shop.
This time I kept my distance
Because a room full of shoes had dropped.

She asked me to roll down my window.
I opened it a crack.
She asked if she could get in with me.
I said I'm gone and I won't be back.

Chorus:

2nd Bridge:

She loves me in a way that you never did.
She loves me with a passion that you always hid.
Is it a surprise that she is with me now?
Isn't it strange that you refuse to take a bow?

Is it any wonder that nothing ever changed?
Is it any wonder new plans were arranged?
Is it any wonder you walked off the stage?
Is it any wonder you made your own cage?

Chorus:

Close:

It don't look like rain to me.
No sir ree.
No sir ree.
It don't look like rain to me.
Ain't nuthin' comin' down.

It don't look like rain to me.
No sirree.
No sir ree.
It don't look like rain to me.
Ain't nuthin' comin' down.

NOTES: I wrote the first six lines to the first verse, half of the chorus, and half of the bridge in 10 minutes on 12-5-15 after working from the title alone –"Limits to Her Love." I spoke the phrase in conversation and recognized it as a good song title. The rest of the work came through two days later from 10 to 11 a.m.

SUNDAY LUNCH

Dad eats beef for lunch every Sunday like clockwork.
Mom puts the roast in the old GE oven after returning from church.
It is late morning on a Sunday in the fall.
This Week in Pro Football is on TV.
By mid-afternoon the beef is done,
Covered in onions, simmering and sizzling in its own beef juices.
It fills the small, humble but neatly appointed house with its aroma.
Dad carves the beef expertly, thinly sliced.
This done, the antique blue plate with wagon wheels and winter scenes is
Summoned from the cupboard.
Dad carefully, proudly, lays each slice of beef onto
The plate until it is brimming with meat, the slices overlapping into
A steaming aromatic display.
Mom heaps the mashed potatoes into a blue bowl that does not match
The meat plate, but no one seems to notice or care.
Dad takes his place at the head of the table.
While Mom makes the gravy in a frying pan,
Using flour and the beef juice, Dad selects the most succulent slices.
Driven with anticipation, he places them onto his plate amid
A roll, a slab of butter, green beans, potatoes and a gravy chaser.

Their son must be called from the adjoining living room.
Despite his own hunger, the NFL Game of the Week has his attention.
Sunday has from time immemorial been the day of the beefeater.
Happy the man who can call Sunday his own.
He rises to the smell of roast beef
So hearty and mouth-watering it is deafening.
When he's done eating Dad finds his way to the couch.
Mumbling about what a pig does after eating, he says he's had enough.

NOTES: Autobiographical yes. This was my household when I was a kid, and that kid watching football was me. If I was 12 or 13 odds are good I had money on those NFL games. There was a guy who ran a small grocery store who was also a bookie. His son, a buddy of mine, would bring the betting slips to math class each Thursday. You had to have your lunch money bet down by end of day Friday. A few times I included my 'raking leaves' and my 'cutting grass' money. I won the pot a few times, picking the winner in 12 games. The payout was surprising. Then I lost. And then I lost again. I still had money in my pocket when, at the age of 13 I walked away from the sports gambling table. And I never went back. But to this day you can ask me almost anything about the NFL teams from the late 1960s and the early '70s and I'll tell you which team is the best bet.

When I wrote "Sunday Lunch" I used free verse to focus on sound, intonation, alliteration, and diction. I was working on the language as an end in itself to find a voice. There's no music to this nor is rhythm a significant component. Since then most if not all of my work is much more tightly structured with a defined meter. This is one of only 3 free-verse poems in the entire book. But the desire to tell a story is still present. I include it here to honor my Mom and Dad. This was my Sunday after coming home from Sunday school, which tracked the academic year. If I wasn't in the living room watching the NFL, college basketball, or Major League Baseball, I was on a sandlot playing football or baseball, or I was on a playground playing basketball with my friends from school. As one of thousands of kids aged 7 to 18 who played ball in the hometown of Little League Baseball, I had the not-so-unique early dream of playing pro baseball. But as my near-sightedness grew worse that dream became more distant. My other dream was to be a singer and a songwriter. As of this writing that dream is still alive. But I'd still love to get an at-bat in MLB.

SIDEBAR: Catch me a fish. I eat for a day.
Teach me to fish. My hunger's at bay.
Catch me a dream. I see to tomorrow.
Teach me to dream. No thoughts will I borrow.   - M.A.I.

This is me at 13 doing what I loved best at the time -- playing baseball. Mom and Dad both worked so they couldn't always get to see me play ball. But whether baseball, football or basketball from Sunday to Sunday, something good would be waiting in the kitchen when I got home. And it was always cool to get in uniform and go play ball on a day usually reserved for church and Sunday school.

THE BARBER

Tastykakes and lollipops at
The barber shop, the barber shop.
Fried clams and devilled ham at
The barber shop, the barber shop.

An unfixed hole from a bee bee gun
Let in the light from the noonday sun.
Beyond the glass door to the world outside,
Cars and trucks would rumble by.

"Hullo Fred, whaddya say?"
"Not much, Ang. It's a helluva day!"
"How's the boys? Doin' good in school?"
"They're doin' all right, they know the rules."

The barber lifts the apron
From the arm of the barber chair,
And whisks it over the customer
With a crisp and professional flair.

He takes scissors in one hand
And taps them to a comb.
Then sets to trimming and clipping
Another receding, thinning dome.

Instruments of the trade
Move in knowing, sinewy hands
With the grace and precision
Of a conductor's commands.

A child enters the shop, brooding and gray,
Then he solemnly sits preparing for the fray.
"Yer next!" the barber says with a bespectacled grin.
The boy approaches slowly and from his pocket pulls a fin.

"You don't have to pay me
Until I've cut your hair.
Now put away your money
And climb into the chair."

"My Ma said I should pay you first
'Cause last time I forgot.
Since Dad died we ain't got much money.
Ma said we ain't even got a pot..."

"That's all right," the barber told the urchin,
And the boy climbed into the chair.
The barber's smile never dimmed as he
Clipped and snipped and buzzed and buffed
and trimmed the tike with care.

In a whoosh the apron lifted
And the little boy opened his eyes.
For the first time he heard the radio
And it sounded soothing and nice.

"What kind of music is that?" the boy asked.
"It's from a long, long time ago."
"How long, like when you were a boy?"
"Yeah, maybe so, maybe so."

The barber glanced at the boy,
Then at the child's reflection.
Facing mirrors showed little boys to infinity,
And for all of them, the barber had affection.

"Whaddyadoin' for lunch?
You wanna have lunch with me?"
"That'd be great!" the little boy cried.
That'd be a real treat!"

Tastykakes and lollipops at
The barber shop, the barber shop.
Fried clams and devilled ham at
The barber shop, the barber shop.

NOTES: I originally wrote this poem on Dec. 27, 1983, as a gift to my father, who was the barber. This was another early effort of mine uncovered from notes and files. I read it to Dad then to mixed reviews. Literary references? Other than a hint of Dr. Seuss with the first and last stanzas, none save the Beatles, realized long after I wrote it. John Lennon and Paul McCartney's classic song "Penny Lane" has a barber as a character in one verse, and "Fixing A Hole" tells of a metaphorical hole in a roof that allowed rain to get in. But nothing came in through the bee bee gun bullet hole, except refracted light that bent as through a prism. At certain hours of the morning it would produce the colors of the spectrum.

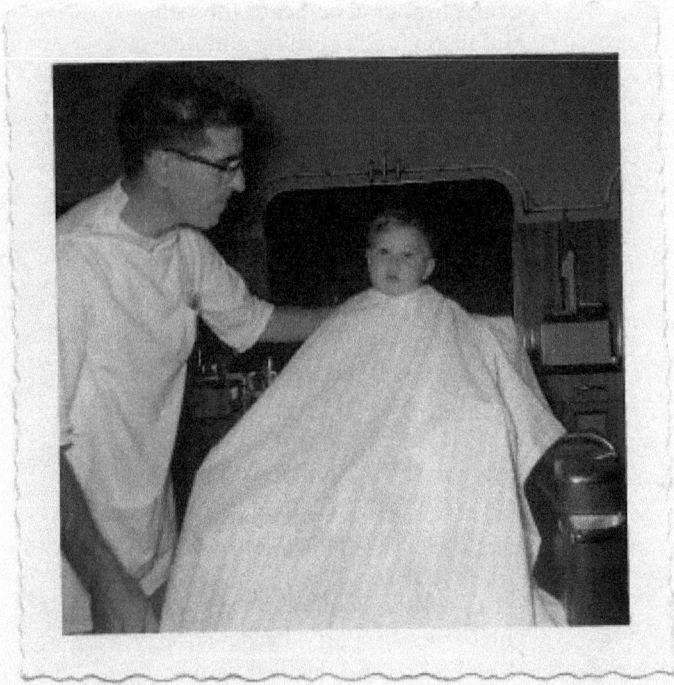

This was my first haircut given to me by my Dad, The Barber, when I was barely 1 year old. My Mom took the picture. I wasn't too sure about what was going to happen at first, and I could never sit still. But in the next frame you can see a look of elation on my face when we were done.

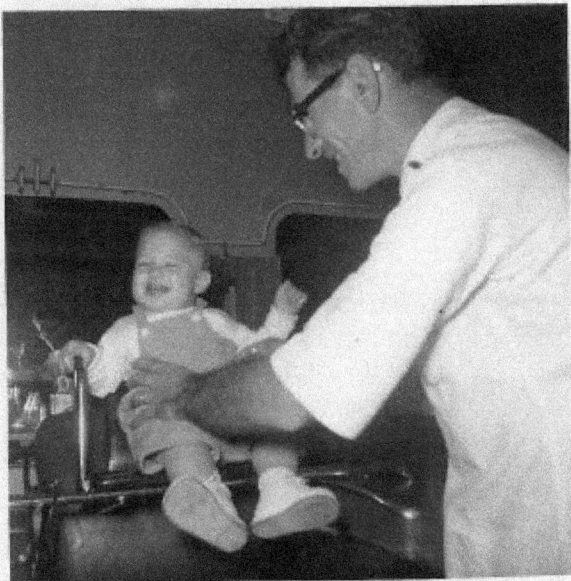

When your father is the best barber in town, it's expected that you are always clean-shaven and that you have a neat haircut. When I was a teenager in the mid-1970s my hair was anything but. I'll never forget getting a haircut one Saturday afternoon at Dad's shop. It was early fall, and as a starter on the Williamsport Area High School football team I had a home game that night. Mom was after me to get a haircut so I looked nice. I said "Ma, no one looks nice. We wear helmets. We're football players." But she insisted I get a haircut. So I rode my bike to the shop and reluctantly plunked myself down into the chair. As Dad would cut, I would interrupt and say things like "Can you not take that much off the top and the sides." It was the equivalent of a back seat driver with a bad attitude. Halfway through, literally, Dad had enough. "Get out of here!" I was so mad I forgot my bike and I proceeded to walk home. On the way I passed the house of a very pretty girl I went to school with who was in the color guard with the school band, and who happened to be sitting on the front porch with her mother. "Hi Michael, how are you?" "Oh, hey Sandy, how you doin'?" Her mother said "Is that Michael? Well, how are you, dear?" I had to turn my head to respond, and when I did she exclaimed "Oh Good heavens! That boy has half a haircut!" Embarrassed as only an adolescent could be, I picked up my pace and muttered "See you later, Sandy." We lost the football game. After I got home that night I apologized profusely to Dad. He opened the shop the next day on a Sunday to finish the haircut for me. Lesson learned, I didn't say a word.

WE DARED

Once long ago,
I held you near.
We shared a moment
Without any fear.

Then you were gone.
I hadn't a clue.
What had I done
To make you so blue?

If you had known
The way that I felt,
You'd be by my side.
Your heart just might melt.

Or would you laugh
In your sunny blonde way,
And be happy inside
That you slipped away?

Sometimes we'd talk
'Till a quarter to three.
With that little-girl look in your eyes,
I knew it was for me.

Bridge:

I never knew a love that felt so right.
Is that why you held my hand so tight?
Moonlight softly fading,
Shooting stars cascading,
A love light in your eyes,
I held you close under velvet skies.

We'd walk through the campus
Holding hands as we went.
I remember those moments,
And the letters you sent.

Once in a dream
You were mine for a night.
Who would believe
Such a heavenly sight?

Then you were gone.
Your feelings turned cool.
I walked alone.
I played the fool.

Where are you now?
Are you with him?
Am I just a memory,
Distant and dim?

Or do you remember
The love that we shared.
Have you any regrets?
Are you glad that we dared?

NOTES: I found this work among my notes and lyric poetry files, written while at Temple University in the spring of 1985. I had answered an ad posted on the music department's bulletin board for a lyricist. The pianist I met could play well from a technical standpoint, but her ear for writing music and her musical influences were far different than mine. She asked me to write a romantic song, so I searched my memory and came up with "We Dared." I presented it to her for her to set to music and I never heard back. As an early effort I thought it had a nice internal rhythm, and the meter was solid. Sometimes simple is best -- four-line stanzas to connote love, love lost, and love remembered with a decent bridge in between.

TACIT AFFINITY

1st Verse:

They had a connection.
They felt it from the start.
A tacit affinity
That springs from the heart.

He saw it in her eyes
And she saw it in his glance.
He knew she was the one
When they started this dance.

She's a very reckless girl.
He's a very cautious man.
Stolen afternoons,
Try to hook up when they can.

Everyone she knows
Just drowns in nine to five.
All she's lookin' for
Is a way to survive.

Chorus:

This tacit affinity,
It runs like a train.
Can't stop it with a brake,
Can't tame it with a brain.

Gotta have her day and night,
There's no time to explain.
This tacit affinity,
It drives him insane.

Her touch is electric,
Her movements sublime.
He reads all her thoughts,
He aches for her time.

She's a hawk on a wire
He's a mouse on the ground.
She's gonna take him higher
To her whims he is bound.

2nd Verse:

He wasted the morning
And prayed for a break.
She polished her nails
And had a piece of cake.

He tasted like coffee,
She smelled of cigarettes.
He took her out to lunch
And they might be there yet.

But the company called --
There's someone he's gotta meet.
He hoped no one knew.
He tried to be discreet.

She laughed when he left and
Took another sip of gin.
Three martini lunch –
You know you'll never win.

Chorus:

Bridge:

She's never where she's says she'll be
But she comes when he calls.
If he ever gets down, if he's ever up a tree,
She's catches him, catches him, catches him when he falls.

A wise man forgives,
And a foolish man forgets.
A woman scorned remembers.
She will tear your heart to bits.

3rd Verse:

She's a very plastic girl
Who straight-up must be seen.
She's a very sexy girl,
The kind that can make you mean.

They have no illusions.
They know the stakes in this game.
They have no parameters.
But only one will take the blame.

They had a connection
They felt it from the start.
A tacit affinity
That springs from the heart.

He saw it in her eyes
And she saw it in his glance.
He knew she was the one
When they started this dance.

Chorus:

Repeat and fade

© 2012, Michael A. Incitti

NOTES: I wrote this in late August and early September 2012. "Tacit Affinity" came from an amalgam of sense impressions and ideas, but like a lot of songs I write, it was driven largely by rhythm and the theme once established. There was no model for this or inspiration, only word play and a back beat rhythm playing in my mind. I entered this work in an ASCAP-sponsored songwriting contest in Nashville in November 2012. A few months later via email I discovered the song had come close to an honorable mention, but it did not win. They said, be happy, we never tell songwriters about the results. I said thanks, but happy doesn't pay the bills.

ZEITGEIST

Intro:

Look at my life.
Is my life OK?
I'll post tomorrow
What I did today.

Everyone can see
I'm an open book
See how I live,
Come take a look.

Anybody I meet
Is a click away.
You can be my friend online,
And see everything I say.

1st Verse:

I got no time
To really get to know you.
But take a look at my life,
Gonna tell you and show you.

This is what I do
For the world to see.
It's all about numbers
And self-flattery.

I really don't know
Too many on my page.
But they're here anyway
As a name and a face.

I measure my esteem
By my number of connections.
I'm an extrovert, you see,
That's my predilection.

Some may call it shallow.
And some may call it lame.
But to me it's who I am.
To me we're all the same.

We all want recognition
For what we say and do.
Even if we do nothing,
We want the world there too.

My life's an open book
Because, truth be told,
No one else will pay attention,
And I don't want to just get old.

Everybody wants to be a hero.
Everybody wants to be a star.
Most keep fiddling like Nero,
And get a mid-life crisis of a car.

Bridge:

The other day I pumped some gas,
And then I bought some candy.
Saw someone I thought I knew
And had my cell phone handy.
So I snapped a pic and posted it.
People liked what I had done.
Can't really say it's crazy
'Cause I'm not the only one.
We're all prisoners of our natures,
Products of our time.
We're bent and shaped like silly putty.
Our whims change on a dime.

2nd Verse:

This is what we do
This is how we live.
It's a function of society
We have no more to give.

Long as they like me
I'll be OK.
It's a little slice of fame
To get me through the day.

It's a superficial world
With my personality on display.
Affirmation, justification,
Self-worth on its way.

It's a sign of the times,
It's the spirit of the season.
A personal yearbook
Without rhyme or reason.

It's a book about faces
And why their lives matter.
A billion worldwide
With illusions to shatter.

They all have their motives
Somewhere on the scale.
They all have an agenda.
They know they can't fail.

They all post their lives
For strangers to see.
To say 'My life is better,
I hope you agree.'

They don't sing or dance,
The young they don't teach.
They don't write great works,
They don't cure disease.

Bridge 2:

It's built in the race
To look at a face.
Piaget breaks it down into blocks.
You can look all you want,
And maybe even flaunt.
You'll get an OK from Dr. Spock.

It's the basis of attraction,
Help you find some satisfaction
In a world that doesn't always understand.
We have our eccentricities,
We're not inventing electricity,
We're just doing what our egos demand.

3rd Verse:

Most are ordinary people
Living ordinary lives.
Trying to live within their worlds,
And to overcome their lies.

It's reversion to the mean
By an exponent of ten.
Generation after generation
Will do it all over again.

Outro:

Look at my life
Is my life OK?
I'll post tomorrow
What I did today.

Everyone can see
I'm an open book.
See how I live.
Come take a look.

Anybody I meet
Is just a click away.
You can be my friend
For at least a few days.

NOTES: I wrote "Zeitgeist" on 8-23-13 from 3:51 a.m. to 5:10 a.m. in longhand on a small notebook. I awoke from sleep with the first eight lines in my head, then the next 4 lines came, (the Intro and the Outro) so I thought I'd better get up and write it all down before I fall back to sleep and forget the lines. Once I started writing, the lines and the stanzas kept coming. I edited the work that day and wrote the second bridge from 12:20 to 12:30 p.m. over lunch. Because of the elemental psychological aspect of it, the Piaget line came to me. Once I had 'block' I had to rhyme it with 'Dr. Spock,' another noted child psychologist, in keeping with the established undertone. The result is a satirical look at Facebook, the social network phenomenon that to date boasts 1 billion users worldwide. From an observational standpoint, Facebook is really social psychology and psych 101. There's nothing tricky about it. Facebook is for and about people who create an online version of their own not-so-private, real-time scrapbook. The present work was in fact inspired by some people I know who virtually live their lives on Facebook. The original title was Bookface, an inversion of Facebook through a looking glass darkly. But "Zeitgeist"—German for "spirit of the times" -- is a more effective, more comprehensive title. It is global in scope like Facebook itself, and more descriptive as social commentary. As of this writing I am not on Facebook, but that's more a function of my lack of time because of my prevailing interests. Published accounts suggest there are psychological side-effects to using Facebook on a recurring basis that for some are clearly negative. But I suppose this is a collateral aspect that is a part of any social system, even one that exists in cyber space. In sum and in fairness, Facebook does a lot of good in the world simply by bringing people together and by keeping them in touch with each other. And my business sense tells me that its template and core business model will only get stronger over time. So long live Facebook.

CHAPTER 6
PERSPECTIVES

ANOTHER DAY

1ˢᵗ Movement:

Sometimes she wonders why her dreams are so far away.
It doesn't matter that much, she hears herself say.
Then she remembers we're all just searching to find our own way.
We're trying to find our own way.
Long as there's love in her heart she'll have strength for another day.

2ⁿᵈ Movement:

She is always reaching far beyond the stars.
Looking for a light so she'll know where you are.
Her days are so long she can hardly see the end.
The night plays her songs, they can be her only friend.
You can't make her over into something that she's not.
All your empty promises get tied up in a box.
Morning comes, the box is filled; it's stuffed with paper dolls.
Lessons from another life, still no one ever calls.
Then sunlight shines through the gray.
It chases clouds away.
She slips on her coat and she starts another day.

3ʳᵈ Movement:

She drives herself to places no one ever sees.
Takes all she's got and then it brings her to her knees.
Now she has no secrets to betray.
Now she knows there's nothing more to say.
She gave it all away.
There's just one place left to stay.
Until morning comes, she awakes,
And she greets another day.

Instrumental Bridge:

Bridge:

Now she sees the light.
God's love shines so bright,
Bright as the midday sun,
On the wings of doves,
Carried from the clouds,
Archangels singing loud,
Radiance beaming all around.
Now she knows just what she's found.

Repeat 1st Movement

Sometimes she wonders why her dreams are so far away.
It doesn't matter that much she hears herself say.
Then she remembers we're all just searching to find our own way.
We're trying to find our own way.
Long as there's love in her heart she'll have strength for another day.

NOTES: Just as "Another Day" has 3 movements, the overall construction and refinement of the song had several movements along its journey to completion. The music to the first movement came first with this song. It came in bursts on 12-3-13 and 12-6-13. On 12-7-13 the lyrics came and I revised the music to fit the lyrics, which tightened the overall rhythm and structure. Two weeks later on Christmas Day late at night I further refined the music and lyrics to the second movement. Over the next two days I completed the third movement in its entirety. I added a musical introduction on 12-30, a closing piano interlude leading back to the 1st Movement, and a bridge.. The words to the bridge bring into focus the underlying message of the song – trust that God will help you find your way, no matter what your struggle. The song is somewhat sad in its description of the main character, but the song is uplifting in the end because it reflects the strength and resilience of the human spirit to carry on in the face of adversity.

ENOUGH ROPE

Coffee's cold.
The day is old.
It's six o'clock.
The door is locked.
Punched a creep.
Can't get no sleep.
Dropped by to say I'm leaving.
Heard it all before.
Words fall on the floor,
Like rocks that can hurt.
They're yesterday's dirt.
Kick 'em under the carpet,
A dinosaur tar pit.
No one here will be grieving.

2nd Verse:

Enough rope
Hanging on soap.
Wash the stain,
Roll it down the drain.
Another arrives
Like bees to a hive.
You just don't understand.
I will listen
Until your eyes glisten.
Bones turn to dust.
Leave if you must.
Don't say goodbye.
I know you won't cry.
You can always take my hand.

Chorus:

All the choices you made are your own.
I would not push you away.
I tried to help you, to give you a home.
But you never had anything to say.

You ride a path of least resistance
Toward an uninspired end.
You choose a tack of false persistence,
With one who's not your friend.

Bridge:

I was there when it all began.
You chose every step of the way.
There was writing on the wall,
You would not wait another day.

Now sorrow follows you
Like a restless wolf in the snow.
How many times will you go back
Before you finally know.

2nd Verse:

Enough rope
Hanging on soap.
Wash the stain,
Roll it down the drain.
Another arrives
Like bees to a hive.
You just don't understand.
I will listen
Until your eyes glisten.
Bones turn to dust.
Leave if you must.
Don't say goodbye.
I know you won't cry.
You can always take my hand.

Chorus:

3rd Verse:

She's a serious dog
With tireless legs.
She's a monkey who drinks
The wine to the dregs.
With nothing to hold
And to never be held,
The flames of time
Will forge and weld.
The human heart
Becomes a box of tin.
Nothing comes out,
Even less gets in.

NOTES: This work came in bursts on 1-10 and 1-11-14. I merged the two outputs on 3-10-14 for their thematic consistency and the natural close that the 3rd verse provides. It was not a planned work; it occurred spontaneously and demanded to be written. It is somewhat experimental in design with extremely short phrases and fragments for added effect.

HISTORY RHYMES

Chorus:

Please tell me why the baby cried.
Tell me why he couldn't sleep.
Tell me what lies on the other side.
Please tell me what I can keep.

I know that every generation
Owes a debt to the one that went before.
Time after time, and life after life,
We walk through the very same door.

Like his dad, the son became a pilot.
Flew a helo and could stop on a dime.
The past rarely repeats itself,
But sometimes history rhymes.

1st Verse:

His father met his mother through the DOD.
They danced at the USO.
Flew his Hellcat through the eye of a needle,
Then they took a three-day blow.

Dietrich, Garland, Grable and Shore.
The grunts in the front don't care what she wore.
Crosby, Astaire, Benny and Hope.
You're in the Navy, you won't meet the Pope.

They got married in '45,
Their son came along in '49.
Took after his dad in every way –
A pilot by design.

Chorus:

2nd Verse:

The '60s came with Vietnam.
The son wanted to enlist.
The draft got him, but he didn't mind.
The Air Force couldn't resist.

Things got rough in '68.
There was fighting all around.
He flew his Huey through the eye of a needle,
And he saved everyone on the ground.

Then one day toward the end of his tour
He volunteered to fly supplies.
He delivered the meds while the enemy waited.
On his way back they shot him down from the sky.

Bridge:

Bricks and mortar, nails and wood.
A home is built to last.
Flesh and blood and brittle bones,
We all become the past.

We tend our lots with care and grace.
Our soil is rich and brown.
We grow our lives at breakneck pace,
Until our planes come down.

Epilogue:

Now they visit him at Arlington.
They touch his name upon a wall.
His mom and dad knew some wouldn't make it back.
But they still wonder why their boy had to fall.

Chorus:

Please tell me why the baby cried.
Tell me why he couldn't sleep.
Tell me what lies on the other side.
Please tell me what I can keep.

I know that every generation
Owes a debt to the one that went before.
Time after time, and life after life,
We all walk through the very same door.

Like his father the son was a pilot.
Flew a 'copter and could stop on a dime.
The past doesn't always repeat itself.
But sometimes history rhymes.

© 2014, Michael A. Incitti

NOTES: The title "History Rhymes" came to me in late January. I wanted to write another anti-war song about successive generations going to war, but I had only a rough framework of ideas. The title comes from Mark Twain's often-repeated phrase that "History may not always repeat itself, but it often rhymes." On 1-27-14 from 3 to 3:20 p.m. the first eight lines and final two lines of the refrain came to me. Then I left my office and my piano to get to a basketball game to referee. I also wrote the music to the chorus on this day, and as I walked onto the court the music was still playing in my mind. After some editing the lines to what became the bridge came to me at 4:27 a.m. on 3-10-14. After I wrote the bridge, the rest of the story came through. With the help of 6 of my wife's chocolate chip cookies and a pot of coffee it was done by 11:30 a.m. I did research on the USO during WWII, and on aircraft during WWII and Vietnam. I think this poem results in a touching story, and unfortunately in the case of the fictional son, one that was repeated too often in the reality of war in the late 1960s. It was good to finish this song lyrically from concept to finished product. A week later I wrote the music. It's a bright, cadenced sound in major keys, and then minor keys depicting sorrow overlaid with duty. It brings a tear to my eye. Sometimes I berate myself for getting emotional over something I've written. Then I'm reminded of what poet Robert Frost said: "No tears in the writer, no tears in the reader."

I MET SOMEONE

Intro:

I met someone.
It happened quite by chance.
I met someone.
She offered me this dance.
You see, I met someone.

1st Verse: I tried to resist,
But her eyes did persist.
I couldn't walk away.
She didn't have to say
A word.

I held her in my arms,
I was captured by her charms.
There was no one else around,
Two hearts beating to the sound,
We heard.

Chorus:

I met someone.
It happened quite by chance.
I met someone.
She offered me this dance
You see, I met someone.

I met someone.
It surely wasn't planned.
I met someone.
One look she took my hand
And then I met someone.

2nd Verse: It's hard for me to tell you
Just what's on my mind.
All my words escape me.
I'm not the wandering kind.
You know.

But you and I, we never walked together.
Alone with you, I could not see forever.
I grew tired of your lies.
Few hellos and more goodbyes,
It shows.

She glanced and caught my eye.
It's a fact I can't deny.
There was always something missing,
When you and I were kissing.
I met someone.

Chorus:

Bridge:

These are the words you didn't want to hear.
This is the look that was never very clear.
Venus and Mars didn't take us very far.
The night never showed us that shooting star.

Sometimes you get what you want.
Other times you get what you need.
I'm crazy for this girl. She's my laughter, she's my pearl.
She's everything to me, ice cream skies on a blueberry sea.

Chorus:

3rd Verse: I took her out for coffee
And we might just be there still.
We had to get to work.
Her smile eased the morning chill.
I met someone.

I hope you understand.
I have no sad regrets.
Once more I'll hold your hand,
But tonight you must forget
Because I met someone.

Now you tell me that you met someone too.
Your heart is ready to start something new.
The truth is in my eyes, my smile cannot hide.
It's the only time to you I ever lied.

Chorus:

You met someone.
It happened quite by chance.
You met someone.
He offered you this dance.
I see, you met someone.

Chorus:

Repeat and fade....

NOTES: I wrote this at 7:30 a.m. on a rainy morning at Wegman's café in Wilkes-Barre, Pa., 12-4-13. I had taken my wife to work because her car was in the shop. I stopped in for coffee and the words just came to me. So I sat down and wrote them in the dark and empty cafe. The music in A flat came to this work on Christmas Day 12-25-13, and a few more lines of lyrics. Lyrics were further refined on the morning of 1-22-14, with a final stanza added on 2-9. For this song I was going for a 1940s or 1950s feel, something that Frank Sinatra or Dean Martin might have sung. I added the final stanza for literary effect with the protagonist's ex-girlfriend meeting someone new also. Accordingly, the words to the refrain become "You met someone...." It is definitely a Sinatra-type song with piano accompaniment. There was no person as an inspiration. The idea for it probably came from reading an article about body language in man-woman relationships. The rest was word play and narrative progression.

SHORT LEASH

Chorus:

Canyons of concrete,
Icons of steel.
No one knows what you think,
No one cares how you feel.

1st Verse:

Each night you try to sleep,
But all you do is toss and turn.
You try in vain to remember
All the silly things you learned.

Knowledge alone
Won't get you relief.
The night may be endless,
But time is still a thief.

You're on a short leash.
Today you're my bitch.
Tomorrow is a slow feast,
Then the roles we will switch.

The corporation is the thing,
It's the center of our universe.
For a pittance it will make you sing.
Could they treat you any worse?

Never any fun or spontaneity,
Nor happenstance guided by design.
No exploration of possibility –
Why can't you read between the lines?

There's a sadness that we live with
More than dreams unfulfilled.
There's a madness that pervades our lives
Like streams through rolling hills.

Chorus:

Canyons of concrete,
Icons of steel.
No one knows what you think.
No one cares how you feel.

2ndVerse:

When you take that ride
To the thirty-ninth floor
You meet a guy behind a desk
Who's heard it all before.

Got your business blue suit
And your hundred-dollar tie.
All the numbers are crunched --
You know they never lie.

They greet you with a smile
And they tell you have a seat.
Corporation makes a change,
Now you're out on the street.

Got your stuff in a box,
And your files on the floor, man.
On the way back down
You can't even trust the doorman.

Train ride home makes you
Think about your wife.
Is she in it for the money?
Will she find a new life?

The children are young
They'll learn to adjust.
They just started school.
Now who will they trust?

Chorus:

Canyons of concrete
Icons of steel.
No one knows what you think,
No one cares how you feel.
3rd Verse:

Dying on a vine,
Wilting in the heat,
Evaporating hopes,
You can't fucking breathe.

You don't know
What tomorrow will bring.
But the challenge of today
Lands your ass in a sling.

You're sick of your house,
You're sick of the mess.
You're tired of dealing
With constant distress.

There's no place to sit,
No place to rest,
No time to think,
No time to guess.

No respite from the noise
And the echoes of anger.
They lay around waiting
In suspended languor.

There must be a way
To overcome this plight.
Should you turn away and run
Or should you stand pat and fight?

Chorus:

Canyons of concrete,
Icons of steel.
No one knows what you think,
No one cares how you feel.

Epilogue:
Some will give,
And some will receive.
But once you begin
There is no reprieve.

Best you can do is
One day at a time.
Make sure corporate life
Doesn't lead you to crime.

Chorus:

Canyons of concrete,
Icons of steel.
No one knows what you think,
No one cares how you feel.

NOTES: This poem came in pieces over a matter of weeks in July and August 2011. It began with the chorus. What followed then had to be put together like a puzzle drawn tight by a thematic string -- dissatisfaction with the often exploitative nature of corporate life. Once I knew what the story was about, the verses fell into place. This work arose from a fragment of a conversation. I overheard the 39th floor line while waiting to board an elevator at a corporate headquarters in Philadelphia. A guy in a blue suit lamented having to take the elevator to learn of his corporate demise. I liked the line and the timing was good. It was consistent with the theme of the beleaguered corporate everyman, and it shaped tone, mood and diction for the present work.

This is me in corporate garb. I could look the part, but that was never me. For many, the dichotomy of corporate life is that you're surrounded by people all the time, but it can still be a very lonely place with a diminishing trust factor as you ascend a hierarchy. I much prefer working with a small group of good friends, or a couple of trusted colleagues. One person with a great idea is a powerful force. Two people with that same idea can be a juggernaut.

HAVE YOU EVER BEEN IN LOVE?

Chorus:

Have you ever been in love?
Have you ever known the meaning of
Something so rare, nothing quite can compare,
To the feeling of being in love?

Intro.

Love knows no timeline.
It can't be set with a dial.
Love knows no ending.
Once begun it continues to beguile.

Love is everlasting
Through all that life can bring.
Love is ever-gracious.
It lifts you up and makes you sing.

Have you ever been in love?
Have you ever known the meaning of,
Something so rare, nothing quite can compare,
To the feeling of being in love.

1st Verse:

Long ago I saw her,
And my mind just won't forget.
Long ago I held her.
That's as close as I would get.

Her deep brown eyes could see forever.
Sometimes I had to look away.
One touch of her hand I was at her command.
When I kissed her I just had to say

Have you ever been in love?
Have you ever known the meaning of
Something so rare, nothing quite can compare,
To the feeling of being in love.

Bridge:

There were a few who had come before.
But there were none who came along after.
The world was right, I beamed with delight,
Whenever I heard her laughter.

Sometimes she wore her heart on her sleeve.
She alone could make the pieces fit.
If I held her again, I knew I'd never leave.
If I wrote her a song, I'd have a hit.

2nd Verse:

Now and then I look at old photographs.
They're never hard to find.
I keep them in my memory
In a room in a corner of my mind.

That's where I see the girl who got away.
She's a bright red rose on a timeless summer day,
In her sneakers with a tan, tennis racket in her hand.
The game must be played; it's time to make a stand.

Have you ever been in love?
Have you ever known the meaning of
Something so rare, nothing quite can compare
To the feeling of being in love.

3rd Verse:

I don't want to wish upon a penny.
I don't want one thin dime.
What I want is her in my arms.
Anything less would be a crime.

I still see her on her front porch waiting.
But she's no longer on Maple Avenue.
I don't know where, but I'll find her there
In that place where love is known by few.

Outro:

Have you ever been in love?
Have you ever known the meaning of
Something so rare, nothing quite can compare
To the feeling of being in love.

Love knows no timeline.
It can't be set with a dial.
Love knows no ending.
Once begun it continues to beguile.

Love is everlasting
Through all that life can bring.
Love is ever-gracious.
It lifts you up and makes you sing.

© 2014, Michael A. Incitti

NOTES: I woke up Thursday morning, March 27, 2014, with the chorus in my mind, "Have you ever been in love? Have you ever known the meaning of something so rare, nothing quite can compare to the feeling of being in love." As with "I Met Someone," I was going for a 1940s or 1950s feel -- something like the timeless lyricist Johnny Mercer might have written. I wrote this song in an hour, 9 a.m. to 10 a.m., and edited it the following morning with work on the bridge. On the 29th I wrote the 3rd verse, then I arranged it all on 3-30 – a very linear progression from start to finish in a tight time schedule. And very rare for me.

PRETZELS, NOT PLUMS

Today I bought the pretzels.
I know I shouldn't have.
But they are so exquisite.
Salty and crunchy with perfect texture.
Texture is important.
The hard pretzels could break your teeth.
But the thin pretzels -- oh so thin, oh so crunchy.
We were at the grocery store.
I stopped in front of the pretzel display.
She had ignored them and passed by.
She knew what I was doing.
Over her shoulder she said "What are you doing?"
I said "Nothing, dear."
I grabbed the bag and placed it in the cart.
She said nothing for two aisles, then
"Why did you get that bag of pretzels?
"You know you're not supposed to eat them."
"You have pretzels. I have pretzels. What?"
Earlier she told me not to ride my bike.
"I don't want you riding your bike at night.
"Someone will run you over."
"I'm careful."
I didn't tell her about the
Dumb-ass woman who nearly ran me over yesterday.
A yellow lab was on the loose, but in her own yard.
This woman drove into the other lane -- My Lane! –
ostensibly to avoid the dog.
But since the dog was in her yard
There was no logic to this so it was
For No Fucking Reason!
I sideswiped a rose bush and escaped harm.
I yelled over my shoulder "You dumb-ass!"
The car sped away.

The quiet streets of the development are well-lighted tonight.
Two skate boarders glide past, nodding as they go,
at ease in their nocturnal world.
The clear night, the chill of late fall, the moonlight,
All give a sense of freedom while I ride. My freedom.
This troubles her. She wants to know about money also.
I tell her the money is taken care of. But still she asks.
Until tonight.
Tonight, after the pretzels, after the bike ride, after the
money discussion,
She finally understands.
So today I bought the pretzels, not plums, pretzels.
And she knew.

NOTES: Two literary influences drove this work: William Carlos Williams, the great poet and physician, who wrote "The Plums" and "The Red Wheelbarrow," and one of my favorite literary giants, Ernest Hemingway. His short story "The Short Happy Life of Francis Macomber" resonates and echoes through the above work with the tension between the husband and the wife. If you read each one of those works, you'll know how this one was built. There is a hint of novelist John Updike present also with dialogue and setting. "Pretzels, Not Plums" was written in my mind during a bike ride from 5:30 to 6 p.m., then on the computer from 6 to 6:20 p.m. on 11-3-14. It is autobiographical in the sense that I ride a bike and that I like pretzels, but otherwise it is inspired by the referenced literature. Free verse works with this subject, a story about change and becoming. Meter and rhyme would be too confining. It doesn't need artifice; it just needs telling.

SLED RIDE

My sister and I rode long ago
On a sled that sped o'er cold, wispy snow.
Those winters are etched in my heart and my mind
Evoking adventures now hard to find.
We flew like the wind, for a moment as one,
Suspended on a course of trials to be won.
The rides were endless down winding slopes,
Though never quite reaching our imagined hopes.

My sister is no longer with us today.
But I remember our joy and laughter through play.
And now each of our children speeds o'er the drifts,
And I hear their cries at a fevered pitch,
As they fly on the crisp and downy white snow,
Bringing lofty memories of rides long ago.

NOTES: I wrote this in 1982 while on the rewrite desk of The Sunday Grit newspaper on a snowy Saturday night. It is somewhat autobiographical, as with any writer drawing from the known or the experiential, but most of it is imagination and extrapolation for effect. The paper published it, and ran a wire photo to go with it of a girl and boy riding on a sled down a snow-covered slope. This was one of many times I would find a unique old wire photo depicting interesting people or scenes and task myself to write a story or poem based on the photograph. Think of a Norman Rockwell-type painting and you'll know what type of subject matter I was looking for. I did this toward the end of the night if there was no news coming in and my work was done and filed. A picture is still worth a thousand words, but in my lyrical exercises I always attempted to bring it in with half that amount. The Grit was based in my hometown of Williamsport, Pa. I was 23, and people in town knew me and my family and they came to follow my byline and my poems. Some asked me about this poem, and one person in particular said he was sorry to hear about my sister. I told the truth that even though it was somewhat inspired by one of my cousins, happily she is still very much alive, and is to me still like a sister.

BALLERINA

From my seat in the balcony
I watched very carefully.
A pretty ballerina danced with ease
Like a soft and silent late summer breeze.

As the ballerina danced her blonde tresses would fly.
Her taut, supple legs would spring, float and glide.
Then a silky pirouette from way up high,
Again and again she would softly alight.

Her white chiffon dress flowed like sunlight to her knees.
She leaped and she flew like a tigress on the trapeze.
A spritely angel capable, without words or speech,
Of bearing a timeless message that runs oh so deep.

From my seat in the balcony
I watched very carefully
And found myself making believe
The ballerina was all for me.

NOTES: It was late July 1979 and I was attending summer school at Bloomsburg State College to get ahead with credits so I would be available for a journalism internship in the fall – which I did not get. I didn't have to work that night so I attended a musical that was playing at Haas Auditorium that featured a ballerina. The musical was "Carousel," one of my favorites. This dancer captivated the audience in her few moments on the stage. The ballerina played the daughter of Billy Bigelow, the protagonist in the play. She appeared to him in a type of dream sequence. That brilliant Rodgers and Hammerstein work is still a monument to the American Musical Theater. When I got back to my apartment that night, I wrote this poem in 30 minutes.

GOODBYE

Lavender and lace adorned your white cotton dress.
To your waist your blonde hair flowed like wine.
I sought in vain for your favors that day.
Though you couldn't stay, you left with a smile.

The promise of what tomorrow might bring
Sang me to sleep and I dreamed
That together on some forgotten beach,
We'd soar like birds of the sea.

Reality struck like an icy winter rain.
I waited but you never came.
Inside a voice kept taunting me
Saying everything's always the same.

It's funny, I thought you were someone,
Someone I might come to know.
Too bad it's just another goodbye
Instead of a fond hello.

NOTES: I wrote "Goodbye" in summer 1979, and with few rhythmic changes or editorial additions this was my work some 36 years ago. Not too shabby for a 20-year old kid. This is another very early work included largely unchanged to serve as a point of comparison between then and now. I wrote the 8-line lyric to "Perspective" on the same day that I wrote "Goodbye." Six years later "Perspective" won a poetry award.

PERSPECTIVE

The portrait of her face is painted and framed
Upon the walls that surround my mind.
I stand in the middle of my gallery
Admiring the beauty of my find.

Through brushstrokes applied with meticulous ease,
Indeed, I sigh, she's one of a kind.
And then I realize, like an artist's dream,
I'd see her if I were blind.
I'd see you if I were blind.

NOTES: This was the first complete lyric I wrote that came to me in a flash. I wrote it in the summer of 1979 (see "Harot's Trilogy"). Despite its elegant simplicity, "Perspective" as an idea came out of nowhere, without rhythm, without music, even without accompanying visual images. I saw the words in my mind's eye. I knew it was a lyric of some type as soon as it appeared, and I always wanted to set it to music. On 3-17-14, from around 9 to 11 p.m., I was experimenting with melody and I came up with 4 bars of music. The following morning, 3-18-14, from 7 to 8 a.m., I wrote the final 4 bars to the song. An hour later I wrote the close. It's in the key of A major. It has a simple, yet powerful message amplified by the bright sounds of several major chords with some minor 7ths thrown in for good measure. With music to carry it, I added the line "I'd see you if I were blind," adding the 'you' to personalize the song as if he's singing directly to her, the object of his ardor. In terms of its relatively brief lyric, it reminded me of Chicago's hit "Color My World." I was very happy at having finally written the music to lyrics I had composed 35 years before. All I could do was thank God, and play the song over and over. "Perspective is just over 2 minutes in length. I play the melody through once with an instrumental bridge, then I play it again while singing the lyrics, then close. Sometimes shorter songs have greater impact.

CHAPTER 7
SONGS IN THE KEY OF THE HEART

RAIN

Instrumental Intro.

1st Verse:

When the rain begins it takes away the golden sun.
Then it brings the clouds and they just rain on everyone.
But you and I,
We love the rain.
We wouldn't have it any other way.

1st Chorus:

We've been through all the rain heaven can send.
I've held you in my arms 'til your heart mends.
Rain may come and rain may go, it brings us back again.
Now we know the meaning of a love that never ends.

2nd Verse:

Think of how it was then.
You were the yin to my yen.
I dropped my books.
You had to look.
I wouldn't have it any other way.

2nd Chorus:

I've held you through ten thousand peaceful nights.
Until stars fade and give way to the light.
You awake from slumber to a morning sun so bright.
Safe again from darkness and the spirits now in flight.

Bridge:

I waited in the park that day.
The rain it came as if to say,
If she means that much to you,
Then your love is true.

I started home, I walked alone.
The rain it poured, my heart was cold.
You pulled alongside, you gave me a ride
Then we knew.

3rd Verse:

Think of all that we've done.
I knew you were the one.
The sun was bright.
My steps were light.
You smiled and I drifted away.

2nd Chorus:

Instrumental Bridge:

Repeat 1st Verse:

1st Chorus:

Repeat Instrumental Intro.

The rain starts and keeps falling down.

Repeat 4 times then close

NOTES: This is a simple song about a man and a woman overcoming life's struggles and challenges with rain as the metaphor. The lyrics are deceptively simple driven largely by the rhythm of the song. The music came first with this song, which I began on 6-9-14 a few days after recording 4 of my songs at a professional recording studio in Clarks Green, Pa., with Dr. Casey Burke, a physician friend of mine who moonlights as a musician and a gifted sound engineer. I had no idea what the subject was, but a few lines of lyrics came to me on 6-10-14 and I wrote them. These comprised the second and third verses. I wrote more music on 6-13, then on 6-15 and 6-16 I wrote the instrumental bridges and the bridge. Working on the song almost all day on 6-16 brought the musical structure into focus. After supper I went to the piano and the first verse came to me.

I knew what the song was about. This verse informed the bridge, which didn't come until nearly midnight on 6-16, but between 8 and 10 p.m. the song was fairly complete, a good Monday. When I thought about what it sounded like I decided the instrumental introduction and some of the verses sounded like raindrops. Because rain can be both good and bad, I chose rain as the metaphor to describe a young couple's experiences, from meeting and falling in love, to going forward to meet life's challenges. It's a lively sound with a beautiful series of chords that evoke rain in various stages. The sound kept compelling me to go back to the piano until it was written. I love this song for its interesting rhythms and its cascading piano riffs. Between 9 and 10 p.m. the need for a second chorus came to me because the designated chorus would be repeated 4 times with 4 verses, and that was too much. The song needed more variety. So I recast lines that originally came to me but weren't immediately used. Informed by the meter of the music, the content of these lines became the second chorus. The song was completed on 6-18-14 with a run time of 4 minutes. This process was very linear and condensed. I wish all my songs came to me that quickly and efficiently. This song is for and about my wife, Aprile and how and when we met. More than anything I ever wrote, it is our story.

"She pulled alongside, she gave me a ride, then we knew...." When she offered me a ride in the rain, it was an offer I couldn't refuse.

UNREQUITED

Intro.

I've been there. You have too.
It's the time that tells when the world is blue.
It's an ocean so deep you think you might drown.
You can't find a lifeboat, you can't see the town.
It's a maze and a web on a one-way street.
It's a very bad dream, and there's no retreat.
It's a pew in the back 'neath the balcony.
You struggle to find semblance of piety.
The faces there all seem to stare, in darkness they are united.
You see her on the aisle -- she's everywhere -- for your love is unrequited.

1st Verse:

Once there was a pleasant fellow
Who was crazy for this girl.
She loved him like no other.
She really rocked his world.
He thought they were an item,
He thought of no one else.
But when she was done with him,
She'd pull another from her shelf.

Chorus:

Unrequited. It's a dirty, rotten shame.
Unrequited. Someone must be to blame.
It was fun to be seduced.
It took a while to deduce.
Now your candle sits without a flame.

Unrequited. You could call it an addiction.
Unrequited. A little wine, a little friction.
There was a time when you thought it was cool.
Now you're stripped and you've been schooled.
The trial is outside your jurisdiction.

Bridge:

Like the priest who lusts for the wife of the mayor.
Like the hunted who avoids the eyes of the slayer.
Like the sinner who bows his head in prayer,
Sweet salvation turns to regret.

Like the caged tiger pacing to be free.
Like the crippled bird who can't fly to the tree.
Like the stallion who runs in the sun by the sea,
We all want what we can't seem to get.

2nd Verse:

I knew a man who once loved a woman.
He said he'd outsmart her at her game.
But she never played, though he lived to stray.
Once she knew she was never the same.
I knew a woman who loved to write.
She gave it everything she could.
She spent all her money, and it sure wasn't funny
When they used her book for firewood.

Chorus:

3rd Verse:

The heart is like a dog that is trained by a bell.
When it rings, he must come running.
Deception is a veil that creates a living hell.
And it can't be lifted by cunning.

The heart is a solitary hunter
That covets what it often gives away.
If all we ask is to be loved,
Why can't those we love stay?

Chorus:

NOTES: "Unrequited" was an assignment I gave to myself because the theme of unrequited love, or anything unrequited, is intriguing to explore in literary form. So I set to work and in a matter of hours over a couple of days' time, 10-29 to 10-31, I had the primary framework built. This was largely an exercise preceded by word play and driven by thematic unity. I wrote three 4-line stanzas while on the beach late afternoon on 10-29. I read it to my wife, Aprile, my most forthright and honest critic. She thought some of the lines were good. This became the bridge. Final editing was done on a Saturday morning, 11-1-14. It's a tighter, cleaner work now. What I like most about this work is that I assigned it to myself as a concept and I brought it to life in a couple of days, much like lyricists and librettists do on Broadway, or in a recording studio.

LITTLE BLACK DRESS

Chorus:

Her little black dress is dangerous.
She knows what she wants to do.
Her little black dress is scandalous.
You'll know when to take your cue.

Her little black dress is delirious.
You must approach with care.
Her little black dress is scurrilous.
A glance soon turns to a stare.

Her little black dress makes you follow her.
You'll follow her wherever she goes.
Her little black dress makes you want her.
In heels she's careful what she shows.

1st Verse:

Early one spring morning as the rain fell outside,
He stopped at the grocery store and led with his eyes.
She happened on the aisle, a striking brunette.
She wore a little black dress and a pink barrette.

Her shape was clear as raindrops on the glass.
He watched her bend over to pick up a pass.
He had no shame; he was trapped in her spell.
Felt like he was falling down a wishing well.

She kept her ring finger hidden from view.
She wanted his attention, didn't care about the truth.
Her movements were graceful, her form sublime.
All she really wanted was a piece of his time.

Chorus:

Bridge:

No words were spoken.
There was never any need.
She knew what she was doing.
She knew what signals to heed.
He's really not a stalker.
He just followed her lead.

For a moment she was vexed,
Didn't know how it would end.
Then she took a phone call
After texting a friend.
He moved forward on the aisle
And disappeared around the bend.

Instrumental Bridge

2nd Verse:

There wasn't enough soap to wash her from his mind.
The store was nearly empty as he slipped on a lemon rind.
He laughed and caught his balance with the cart.
He thought of how well she had played her part.

He made his way to the checkout counter
And as he loaded up his things,
He saw the girl in the little black dress --
She showed her hand without a ring.

She paid the cashier to the penny,
Then she turned to him and smiled.
She said "Let's get some coffee.
"The rain will stop in a while."

Chorus:

Repeat and fade

NOTES: I wrote "Little Black Dress" on the morning of 8-22-14 after an early morning visit to a grocery store in Wilkes-Barre, Pa. My wife's car was getting fixed so I drove her to work. The store, with its dimly-lit café, was a few blocks down the road. This poem sat for 2 months until I re-discovered it on 10-30-14, a few weeks after we moved to Delaware. About 80 percent of it was written in that empty café-restaurant on a gray, rainy, late-summer morning. Do you remember the Gordon Lightfoot song "Rainy Day People?" I'm a rainy day person. It was my kind of day. This song is in 3rd person narrative form as it tells a brief story. But it was really my imagination at work after simple observation. A tableau of the images contained in the poem presented themselves before me as I entered the store. It froze in my mind's eye like a painting. I walked straight to the dark, empty café, took out my notebook and wrote. Months later, what a wonderful surprise to find "Little Black Dress" as a work nearly completed. That's why I never throw away notes or observations.

KATY PERRY

Intro.

I want to marry Miss Katy Perry, I want to take her home.
I want to marry Miss Katy Perry, I want her for my own.

Chorus:

I want to marry Miss Katy Perry
But she doesn't even know that I am here.
Oh, I want to marry Miss Katy Perry
Kiss her hands, her face, her hair and hold her near.

1st Verse:

I'll walk backstage when she's done with her show,
Go up to her and maybe say "Yo."
We'll talk for a while
And then she'll say,
"It's getting kinda late.
"Let's go out on a date."
And I'll say,
"Way ahead of you, babe."

People think it's funny,
I don't want any money.
I just want the whole
Wide world to see
That she's my girl,
What a pearl of a girl.
I want to take her
Everywhere with me.

With Katy by my side
We won't even need a ride.
We can walk through the mall
And take it slow.
We can get a slice of pizza.
"Really nice to meet ya,"
All my friends think I am
Katy's beau.

195

I'll take her to the dance
If she just gives me a chance.
I'd get to drive the Buick
Cause it's clean.
I'll take her out to eat
At a restaurant that's sweet.
In a black dress and heels,
Katy is my queen.
Then I'll say,
"Way ahead of you, babe."

Bridge:

Are you happy you're a star?
Did you think you'd get this far?
Is it everything you dreamed about and more?
When you wake up all alone,
And the night winds seem to moan,
Is it you they call and crawl across your floor?

Yes I am precocious,
But my manners are atrocious
And I hardly ever know just what to say.
But if you take me as I am
No one really gives a damn,
So please be mine if only for a day.

Instrumental Bridge:

2nd Bridge:

Gotta make the scene
Because she's in it.
There's no in-between
Can't wait another minute.

My dear Miss Kate,
Oh please don't hesitate.
We'll make our own fate.
My love will not abate.

Chorus:

I want to marry Miss Katy Perry
But she doesn't even know that I am here.
Oh, I want to marry Miss Katy Perry
Kiss her face, her hands, her hair and hold her near.
2nd Verse:

Her sky blue hair
Really knocks me out.
Her laughing eyes
Make me sing and shout.
I know she's never mean,
Even though I'm seventeen.
There would never be
A word for her to doubt.

Katy can you hear me?
You have no need to fear me.
I would do anything
You ask me to.
I would sail across an ocean.
If you ever got the notion,
I'd walk a sandy desert
Cause of you.

We would never fight
Because you are always right.
You're my Katy girl with hair
And eyes of blue.
Whether you are near or far
I hear your voice and your guitar.
Are all of these vibrations
Really true?

I know you'd never slight me.
I ask mighty Aphrodite,
But I fear all my prayers
Are in vain.
You're off on a tour
So I'll just close my door.
Then you won't see my tears
Fall like rain.

Chorus:

I want to marry Miss Katy Perry
But she doesn't even know that I am here.
Oh, I want to marry Miss Katy Perry
Kiss her hands, her face, her hair and hold her near.

Chorus:

Instrumental Close

NOTES: This song is written in the spirit of early rock and roll with an upbeat, fun sound that recalls the music of the '50s and '60s. It is written from the perspective of a 17-year-old boy who has a crush on popular singer Katy Perry. The song is infused with wistful, whimsical adolescent energy, longing and innocence. I also wrote the music to this song, the second lyrical poem I set to music. I like Katy, and I admire her work, but this was a song that began with the rhyming chorus, "I want to marry Miss Katy Perry, but she doesn't even know that I am here. Oh, I want to marry Miss Katy Perry, kiss her hands, her face, her hair and hold her near." The rhymes and rhythms caught me and I just continued to imagine from the perspective of a teenager. That was in November and December 2010. I rewrote some of the lyrics on 9-29-13, and I hammered down the music on 10-10-13 to make it a complete song that is cohesive and more tightly structured. It's a fun sound, reflecting a teenager's carefree ways, with bright, simple chords that become moody in the bridge, but return to the bright, happy chords of the introduction and the chorus. Run time is about 5 minutes. I also wrote two musical interludes to set off the bridges. This was one of the first complete songs I wrote with music and lyrics, but, like love itself, it took a lot of work to refine. Katy Perry through adolescent eyes is the muse for the song. The music is inspired by two more of my favorite composers, Neil Sedaka and Neil Diamond, but it's not nearly as polished. There's always work to be done. I'm very proud of this work though, not only for its completeness, but because I recognized the need for balance in content and went back to the lyrics to refine them to create the final version lyrically and musically. It tells a somewhat complete story about a slice of life from an adolescent world, and through that window it has a universal appeal. This marriage of music and lyrics works.

MANHATTAN SKYLINE

1st Verse:

Dancin'
All the night away.
Dancin'
In our hideaway.
Dancin'
And no one else is there.
Dancin'
Girl you move so fine.
Dancin'
Got to make you mine
Dancin'
For this to end would be unfair.

2nd Verse:

Glancin'
From my high rise, we're
Glancin'
At the skyline, we're
Glancin'
And no one else is there.
Glancin'
Girl your eyes, they shine
Glancin'
Deep into the night
Glancin'
For this to end would be unfair.

Bridge:

Each night it's the same old painted faces.
Only difference is the fast and lonely places.
Women wearing the latest of fashions,
Gentlemen lose all control of their passions.
And that's
All right.
You're mine
Tonight.

Chorus:

Arm in arm we saunter down Park Avenue,
Looking forward to a cozy rendezvous.
Hoping that the night won't end like all the others.
So blue and empty I'd
Given up my trust so many times before.
I'd stopped wondering if there was really more,
But you, you're something new and I need you.

Structural Note: 1st verse, bridge, chorus; 2nd verse, bridge, chorus; instrumental; bridge, chorus, repeat and fade.

NOTES: I wrote the lyrics to "Manhattan Skyline" in August 1979 at my desk in the bedroom of my childhood home in Williamsport, Pa. I had been working on it for several days in between swinging a sledgehammer at a construction site to earn money for college that fall. These are lyrics to the tune of the instrumental song from the soundtrack to the movie "Saturday Night Fever," 1978. I was 20 years old when I wrote it, but I'm still very proud of the rhythmic and metered accuracy and the lyrics of this song. I have never formally tried to sell my lyrics to the instrumental composer of the song, David Shire, or the music publisher. Odds are they would have no need for my lyrics because the instrumental version was already a hit. But someone may want to record the song using its name recognition with a new variation – my lyrics. The song lends itself to lyrics because it is almost a microcosm of the entire disco movement in one song. The catchy melody and driving disco rhythms reflect an era in popular music. But if you ask me, I like the song better with my lyrics. I can hear the legendary Bee Gees, who wrote the lion's share of the soundtrack to "Saturday Night Fever," rolling with this song. Sadly, two of the Brothers Gibb have passed, fraternal twins Robin and Maurice. But eldest brother and principal songwriter Barry Gibb continues to make music. The "Saturday Night Fever" soundtrack produced 4 number one hits in 1978, all written by Barry Gibb. He also wrote the title track to the movie version of "Grease" in that same time period. Sung by Frankie Valli of the Four Seasons, the song went to number one also. The only other group that can lay claim to having 4 number one songs in a similar compressed time period was The Beatles.

SO MUCH TO SAY

On a clear and chilly night
As winter gave way to spring,
Two people with much in common
Sat and talked about everything.

He thought her face was mesmerizing --
A look from old Hollywood.
She was drawn to his intellect,
And his eyes that saw more than they should.

He found her laughter intoxicating,
Her brown eyes smiling and bright.
His words caressed her like a lullaby.
Something about him seemed so right.

She was coy and engaging.
He was kind and gallant.
She was sweet and revealing.
He was never nonchalant.

They sat in a well-appointed bar
Surrounded by an upscale crowd.
Where a wink and a grin held a thousand lies,
For them it was too lush and too loud.

They sat with their coffee in the middle of it all
As if there was no one else around.
With her knowing how the night would end,
And with him wondering what he found.

But her Ava Gardner and his Frank Sinatra
Were not yet meant to be.
Each had another at home waiting,
Though it wasn't always clear to see.

This night would live as a fable of love
In a moment that was honest and true,
In a place where perfection is often sought but never found,
And in a time when real love is known to few.

On a clear and chilly night
As winter gave way to spring,
Two people with much in common
Sat and talked about everything.

NOTES: I wrote this song on March 13, 2008, from 3 to 4 a.m. by the light of the kitchen stove. I had spent the day at a business meeting in Philadelphia. As always happens I take in a considerable amount of sense impressions, both consciously and unconsciously, at large gatherings. These impressions sometimes play in my mind late at night like random scenes from a film I've never seen, often with fragments of dialogue. But I have no idea where the line "A moment that was honest and true" came from, except to say that this was the line that would not let me sleep. This line played in my mind as a working title, and as I tossed and turned the lines kept coming without visual images. At 3 a.m. I got up and wrote "So Much To Say" in one hour, line by line without changing a word. I wrote it while standing in a corner of the kitchen at the counter top beneath the little light on the kitchen stove. This was a case of writing what the subject demanded, and when the story was told it was done. This work is one of my favorites.

ALL-WEATHER GIRL

1st Verse:

There's a girl at work
Who has it bad for me.
But she hasn't done anything
Inappropriately.

Her face lights up
When I walk into the room.
Skirt rises on her thighs
And her sweater starts to bloom.

She says she's in favor
Of taking it slow,
But I got a couple questions
And I'd really like to know.

Will you walk with me
When the rain is falling down?
Baby can't you see
I will always be your clown.

I'm a really nice fella
And I hope you understand.
Want you under my umbrella.
I'm there at your command.

Chorus:

I want to tell you that I love you
And I'll treat you like my queen.
I want to be there in your morning
When the sun is bright and clean.

My all-weather girl,
Want to take you everywhere.
Gonna drive to your horizon,
Sunlight streaming in your hair.
My all-weather girl,
I'll protect you from the pain.
You can cry on my shoulder
In the soft summer rain.

2nd Verse:

My all-weather girl
Is the one that I adore.
I'll place you on my pedestal
And worship on your floor.

Like a walk in the park
As dusk starts to fall,
Moonlight mirrored in your eyes
Makes my motive seem so small.

You're the only girl
That I ever dream of.
If you wonder what I'm feeling,
You know it must be love.

Bridge:

From your head down to your toes,
Kiss the petals on your rose,
Light the candlestick that glows,
With a love that always shows.

Like Mary Tyler Moore and Marlo Thomas,
Throw your hat into the air and wish upon a promise
That tomorrow will be everything you dream,
But always be aware, you're the island in my stream.

Chorus:

3rd Verse:

When I'm driving in my car
Through the snow, sleet and rain.
She is there by my side
To calm my frazzled brain.

She makes me feel so happy,
And there is no in between.
She makes me want to sing and dance
Like my favorite Kelly, Gene.

Now my all-weather girl
Is with me through the seasons.
I bring her snow in the winter,
And rain without a reason.

Minor Bridge:

If you never take a chance
Then you know you'll never fail.
My all-weather girl
Is the wind in my sail.

Chorus, repeat and fade ......

NOTES: "All-Weather Girl" came in pieces throughout the year and I had
to put it together like a puzzle. The first stanza came in the spring, and
some pieces were fashioned in the summer. By then I had a working title,
which aligned the overall theme. The final pieces came in the fall. Once I
had the direction of the work and I knew what it was about the rhythm
drove it. The references to Mary Tyler Moore and Marlo Thomas are
evocative of strong, unique, beautiful women to underscore the singular
beauty and the touch of whimsy of the girl in the song. Gene Kelly is one
of my all-time favorite entertainers, still one of the greatest, forever "Singin'
in the Rain." The song was not inspired by any particular woman. I was
watching a commercial for all-weather tires and I thought it would be cool
to have an all-weather girl, a metaphor for a girlfriend who is always at your
side no matter what happens. And then I realized I already had one. This is
another one of my favorite songs.

WHEN I FELL FOR YOU

Haven't we met
Somewhere, sometime,
Someplace that I can't remember?
Didn't we meet
One night, one day,
One afternoon in December?
Was a chill in the air?
Was it gray, was it bare?
Were the leaves still falling in November?

Chorus:

That was when I fell for you.
One look, one glance
And I knew it was true.
No other face would I ever see.
I knew then and there
You were the girl for me.

Maybe we met
Perchance, per se,
Perhaps on a bright, sunny summer day.
Didn't we meet
One hour, one minute,
One moment when roses bloomed in May.
The birds began to sing --
These things happen in spring -
You left me no choice but to say

Chorus:

That was when I fell for you.
One look, one glance
And I knew it was true.
No other face would I ever see.
I knew then and there
You were the girl for me.

Bridge:

On a cobblestone street
In the warm summer heat
'Neath a lamplight softly fading,
Through an uptown door,
You make my heart soar,
For your smile I will be trading.

In a cab by a gate,
Where you're going don't be late,
I won't be far behind.
In the city time is fast.
There's no future, there's no past.
Only you can ease my mind.

Haven't we met?
Somewhere, sometime, someplace
Yes, now I remember...

Chorus:

That was when I fell for you.
One look, one glance
And I knew it was true.
No other face would I ever see.
I knew then and there
You were the girl for me.

Repeat and fade......

NOTES: "When I Fell For You" was written in bursts on 3-2-11 from 2:38 to 3:37 a.m., and on 3-3-11, from 8 to 9:30 a.m. It was another song driven by rhythm and cadence, particularly on the bridge. There's no definitive source or back story, just multiple sense impressions and an amalgam of sound, rhythm, and thematic unity, all from my imagination. "When I Fell For You" is one of my favorite songs for its sound, mood, pace and cohesion.

SUMMER BRUNETTE

1st Verse:

1st Verse:

She laughs, the waves roll by,
And summer is easy to find.
Soon September is kind
And fall is here,
I hold her near.
It's time to go.
She ought to know
I love her so.
Oh, why can't she see that look in my eyes?
I have no disguise for her.

I'm just a fool in love.
She's what I'm dreaming of.
I don't know what to do.
My heart is crazy for you.

My summer brunette is just
So unforgettable now,
She's captured my heart.
There's only one thing left to start.

Love can be dangerous.
I'm not mysterious.
My love for you is like
Sunshine on a cloudy day

Bridge:

Once in a dream, I held you close to me.
Once in a dream, you were mine.
One love for me, that's all I ask of you.
One love for me, stars align.

Oh, goddess of love, bring her to me,
'Fore she fades like the warm summer sun.
Oh, goddess of love, listen to me,
I know in my heart she's the one.

The morning sun surrounds her,
Another summer day.
I slip my arms around her.
But I don't know what to say.

Instrumental Bridge:

2nd Verse:

She laughs, the waves roll by
And there's not a cloud in the sky.
Soon September reminds
That fall is near.
But we won't hear.
It's time to go.
She ought to know
I love her so.
Oh, why can't she see that look in my eyes?
I have no disguise for her.

Sand castles hold the waves.
We'll take what summer gave.
She is always in reach.
Our days are still warm by the beach.

My summer brunette is just
So unforgettable now.
She's captured my heart.
There's only one thing left to start.

Love can be dangerous.
I'm not mysterious.
My love for you is like
Sunshine on a cloudy day.

Close:

My summer brunette walks with me,
There's a breeze in her hair.
Now she's my only love,
And I haven't a care.

NOTES: "Summer Brunette" is another rare instance where the music preceded the lyrics. I wrote the music to this song on 3-18-13, but I had no lyrics in mind. All I had, based on the sound of the music, was the idea of an upbeat Sinatra-like song in the musical era of the 1940s or '50s. Plenty of key changes keep the melody moving, but lyrics didn't come to me until I worked from the title alone. I had written the title "Summer Brunette" in my notebook months ago, so technically the song began with a title alone. I liked it. It sat there. Then the music came. Lyrics followed the night after my father passed on 3-24-13. I refined the lyrics on 3-25 to fit the music, and I edited all of it on 3-26. The lyrics probably just rolled out from pure exhaustion on the 24th. But the song, with its happy message of a man and a woman in love at the beach, took my mind off of my father's passing at age 92. I added a bridge between the first and second verses writing the music to the bridge on 4-6-13, and the lyrics to the bridge on 4-7-13. It's a more complete work with more defined movement rather than verse to verse. Once I knew the era of the music I knew the song was about what my father might have felt or said to my mother when they were dating. They used to tell a story about my Mom driving to meet my Dad at Virginia Beach when he had shore leave in Norfolk from the Coast Guard during WWII. I wrote this song with the idea in mind that these were Dad's words to Mom. My wife, Aprile, who was born in the summer, is also a brunette and she too is an inspiration for this song. She and I spend a lot of time at the beach in summer, and these are also my words to her. Either way, the song honors those I love.

My Dad, Angelo Incitti, with his "Summer Brunette," my Mom, Celia, at the end of WWII in Virginia Beach, May 1945. They were both from the "Little Italy" section of Williamsport, Pa., also known as "Hollywood" because of all the good-looking men and woman of Mediterranean descent. Here they look like they might have stepped off a Hollywood studio lot. They were a handsome couple with a strong work ethic that lasted all their lives. Photo taken by a Coast Guard buddy.

The poet casts a line ....into the ocean. Generally I go fishing every day. If I'm not fishing for business clients, I'm fishing for ideas for my next song or poem. So who has the time to actually go fishing? On those rare occasions when I do, it's rarer still if I catch anything noteworthy. Here, my wife Aprile gets a kick out of my catch. Beyond the view of the camera at the other end of my line was a piece of drift wood covered in seaweed. I always have better luck on land.

STATE OF GRACE

She sits with me in a state of grace.
Her ass is flat, but she gives good face.
I really want to take her, but she's always on the move.
You'll never ever cheat her cause she's always in the groove.

She's a very cool chick and she loves the NFL.
She roots for her teams and tells the owners "Go to hell!"
She's a badass date in her heels and her leather.
She'll even throw the football – says it's light as a feather.

Seattle, Arizona,
Carolina, Minnesota,
Green Bay, Washington
And that's her NFC.
Kansas City, Denver,
Cleveland and the Bengals,
Pittsburgh, New England
And the Jets fly free.

You can bet on the ponies.
You can bet on the game.
Rest assured they'll take your money.
You'll be left with just your name.

If you really love the gridiron
You've got to see your team.
Take the girl you like a lot,
And forget the Jim Beam.

Love is a gamble.
And love is a curse.
Love lifts you higher
Than the universe.
You know what it is
And you know what it's not.
You know when it sends you,
And when it hits the right spot.
My money's on her --
She's a Saint with a sin.
Even if I lose
For her I'll take it on the chin.

She wants to love the Lions,
But they hardly ever win.
She tries to watch the Eagles,
But she needs a lot of gin.

She's a very tough chick, and I'd never ever slight her.
When she grabs a cigarette you damn well better have a lighter.
She'll fight for the right to call all the plays.
Any day or night it's a pigskin holiday.

Seattle, Arizona,
Carolina, Minnesota,
Green Bay, Washington
And that's her NFC.
Kansas City, Denver,
Cleveland and the Bengals,
Pittsburgh, New England
And the Jets fly free.

She sits with me in a state of grace.
Her ass is flat, but she gives good face.
She's regal and loyal on the 50-yard line.
We're 10 rows back, and she's all mine.

NOTES: Word play and a lifelong love of NFL football drove this one. It's football and fictional characters with a twist of romance – a touchdown every time. Written Dec. 9, 2015, and completed 1-2-16, in 20 minutes. This song is in the rap genre with rapid tempo, tight construction and a lyrical edge. I've been a Philadelphia Eagles fan for as long as I've been a Boston Red Sox fan, since childhood. I also like the Lions in the NFC, so if you follow NFL football you know where those lines came from. AFC? Jets, Pats, Broncos, and the Dog Pound. I generally root for the underdog.

OVERTURE

If I were to make you an overture,
Would you show me your side that is oh so demure?
It seems we never get to romance.
But if you just give me half a chance

I could show you what love's about,
Make you so happy you'll dance, laugh and shout.
I want to know that it's me in your eyes,
The warmth of your whisper, the hush of your sighs.

Would you believe me if I told you I loved you?
Would you believe me if I told you I care?
Would you ever wonder if I'm always thinking of you?
Would you consider us quite a lovely pair?

Your voice was like a cool summer breeze
That caressed my foolish autumn heart.
A church steeple high above the trees
Told me nothing could keep us apart.

We walked barefoot through a September meadow.
Summer flowers had turned gold, brown and green.
The sun was high in a perfect azure sky,
And your eyes were the bluest I'd ever seen.

Would you believe me if I told you I loved you?
Would you believe me if I told I care?
Would you ever wonder if I'm always thinking of you?
Would you consider this life to share?

Years have passed, winters slip to spring.
With you by my side it seems we've done everything.
But the time I remember most of all
Is when we first met and we started to fall.

So today if I made you an overture
Would you show me your side that is oh so demure?
It still seems we never get to romance
But if you just give me half a chance,
My eternal love you'll see in a glance.

NOTES: For "Overture" I drew on a few select images from long ago memories to write this song, with the majority filled in by extrapolation and imagination. When the first two stanzas came to me I thought I had something. So I searched my memory. The result is a story about a man and a woman with the man looking back and remembering as he tells of his love for his wife in the present. The entire song is a memory that celebrates their love.

I then set to work on writing music to my lyrics. In doing so, I discovered I was compelled to write a tighter song prompted by the puzzles of time sequence that did not sacrifice meaning or intent. If it were not for the music, I may not have picked up the hammer and chisel to sculpt a tighter song. It is a better work with music than it was by itself without the discipline of a musical score. The music is inspired by a few of my favorite composers: Burt Bacharach and Hal David, Carole King and Gerry Goffin, and Barry Mann and Cynthia Weil. I'd like to say my song lies somewhere between "I Say a Little Prayer" and "Take Good Care of My Baby," but that would be overstating it a bit. Still, I like "Overture." It's a nice song that I enjoy playing and singing with a run time of 3 minutes. Suitable for a wide audience, it has enjoyed local play.

CHAPTER 8
ENIGMAS

THE TIME THAT TELLS

I thought we had a connection.
I thought we could be friends.
How was I to know, girl,
Our beginning would be the end

Of a story never to be told,
Of an un-played hand that would too early fold,
Of one too afraid to step away from her mold,
Of a present that doubted what the future might hold.

With so much time and space between us
There's no answer to be had.
Still, I never thought such a bright beginning
Would end on a note so sad.

Chorus:

We've reached an inflection point,
We've come to this juncture,
We're here at this place in time.
I'm all out of answers,
I don't know the questions.
We just can't seem to rhyme.

The time that tells is a clock without hands
That measures and gauges the heart.
Without whistles or bells or wind-shifting sands
It threatens to tear us apart.

The time that tells is a beacon
Lighting a path through the night.
Where pain and doubt wrestle faith and hope
While poets like me try to set things right.

Chorus:

Bridge:

We pass through our days
In rose-colored glasses.
We base our moves
On the schemes of the masses.
We sell our souls
For the price of a token.
We neglect our hearts
Until they are broken.

With so much time and space between us
There's no answer to be had.
I never thought such a bright beginning
Would end on a note so sad.

It's a story never to be told.
It's an un-played hand that would too early fold.
It's about one too afraid to step away from her mold.
It's a present that doubted what the future might hold.

Chorus:

NOTES: This was an exercise in writing to refine a craft and to catch lightning in a bottle. My goal was to produce a tangible work every week. The imagery of the line "The time that tells is a clock without hands" comes from one of my favorite paintings, "The Persistence of Memory" by Salvador Dali. To this day I'm the only person who ever got a C in Intro. to Art at Bloomsburg State College. Why? Because I refused to cheat on the tests. There were 500 people in those classes that filled an auditorium. The classes were conducted on a movie screen. The fact that I'm near-sighted may have had something to do with my inability to discern the finer points of Seurat. For the multiple choice tests people would yell out answers. Some even got up and looked over people's shoulders to copy. I would have none of it. So I sat there on my principles and got a C. I knew nothing of Rembrandt, Degas, or Monet. But I knew Vincent van Gogh from the Don McLean song "Starry, Starry Night," I knew a Picasso when I saw one, and a Dali. He was the guy who painted llamas

THE DAY HAS BECOME THE NIGHT

There's a light inside her window,
In a time I cannot bend.
If I listen to the wind blow
I hear echoes of a friend.

If I could see the past
In another place and time,
I could hold all our yesterdays,
And mold them into rhyme.

This is what God asks of me;
It's the path that I must take.
Without fear or dread of tomorrow,
With no room left for mistakes.

I lie awake for hours
On a pendulum of dreams,
Swaying between dark and light,
Where reality bursts at the seams.

Into another dimension,
Through a door to a golden sun.
A new day dawns with the promise of
A task that's never done.

On a plane where the eternal
Often meets the mundane,
We try not to fly off the handle,
While the lion tends his mane.

In the beginning I saw her through her window
Surrounded by illusions and lies.
Now I know which way the wind blows.
Now I think I know why.

She sits in her corner rocking away.
The tears and the years show on her face.
Once long ago when she was quite young,
She believed in dreams and songs to be sung.

Today she'll search for tomorrow's kiss,
Because yesterday, she says, is an errant wish.
Alone in her chair, her altar of faith,
Sometimes she smiles, but always she waits.

I still see her at her table
'Neath a dim and fading light.
And I know I will never hold her,
For the day has become the night.

I'm just here to say what's in your pocket
I'm just here to help you stay sane.
Grab the chain and open up the locket.
Grab the brass ring and go around again.

I wander these halls, a ghostly apparition.
Clothed in thought and wrapped up tight.
I won't give in to reality, won't bend to superstition.
All I know for certain is the day has become the night.

NOTES: I wrote this piece on 6-28-10 from 1:17 a.m. to 2:18 a.m. I seem to do my some of my best work while most of the world is asleep. I do not know precisely where this came from other than a pure creative and literary impulse. The first stanza came to me and wouldn't let me sleep. So I got up and started writing longhand on my legal pad. When I stopped writing this is what I had, almost verbatim. There are multiple meanings for this work. I won't impose mine on the reader, and I'll leave the elusive "she" in this work to the reader's interpretation also. This work was originally titled "Enigma" because that's exactly what it is.

THE REPO MAN

The repo man comes early on a Saturday,
Comes when it's quiet, comes when it's dark.
The repo man comes and takes what he wants.
He knows where you live, knows where you park.

Driving down a boulevard in stages of decay,
I see burned out beer signs in bars of yesterday.
Up ahead the road opens with a graveyard on the right,
Where souls long forgotten dwell in cold and constant night.

There's a light that won't work
On a table that won't stand
In a room dark and dusty,
Untouched by human hands.

She sits in a pool of sadness
That time cannot penetrate.
Rises slowly from her chair,
In defiance of her fate.

She glances in a mirror at
A reflection with no voice.
Saw a face she didn't know,
But she knew she had no choice.

The lies she told herself,
Are the lies that we are told.
Her friends in high places
Won't let her be sold.

She said 'Don't talk to me.
'You don't know what to say.
'Your eyes can't see
'And there's no time to pray.'

I can see it in her eyes,
She's been telling all those lies.
Like a thousand times before.
And this is just once more.

The repo man comes early on a Saturday,
Comes when it's quiet, comes when it's dark.
The repo man comes and takes what he wants.
He knows where you live, knows where you park.

Be careful of the lies you tell others.
They will come back and cut you like a knife.
Be careful of the lies you tell yourself.
They will fool you and steal your very life.

It doesn't matter what you drive.
It doesn't matter where you live.
What matters most is how you feel,
And what you have to give.

The repo man comes early on a Saturday,
Comes when its quiet, comes when its dark.
The repo man comes and takes what he wants.
He knows where you live, knows where you park.

NOTES: This work came in pieces spread months apart, but the final product was worth the wait. The second stanza "Driving down a boulevard...." came to me while driving past a graveyard off Washington Boulevard in Williamsport, Pa., in August 2011 after visiting my father at a nursing home nearby. I liked the lines so much I called my office and left those lines as a message on the answering machine so I didn't forget them. The work began with the repeated stanza about the Repo Man, which came to me while we drove one of my daughters back to school in Delaware after spring break in March 2011. I saw a red repo truck carting away a black Porsche. It was a cloudy Saturday morning about 7 a.m. We stopped at a restaurant to eat breakfast and I took out my notepad and wrote the stanza that would define the work. I then had scrambled eggs, a slice of ham, wheat toast, and a pot of coffee, my favorites

DEATH ON THE HALF SHELL

Imagine the modest clam, if you will.
He's a seemingly insignificant fellow.
But upon closer look, you'll see he's chilled.
And he's stuffed with an abominable yellow.

The clam never learned how to act, you see.
And his heart is two-dimensional and bland.
His emotions are kept locked up, never free.
So he's plain and predictable as sand.

While we analyze the reclusive shellfish
His hours pass languidly on the ocean's floor.
Many enjoy his halves split on a dish.
Others watch waves wash him to Stygian shores.

Sometimes the clam is snared in a net.
On days such as those it's a pretty safe bet.
He'll end gray and withered on somebody's plate.
Don't we all find a similar fate?

© 1983, 2011, Michael A. Incitti

NOTES: I was working nights on a daily newspaper. I preferred the night shift because there were just a few of us on duty with no one looking over your shoulder. It was generally quiet, except for the occasional hum of the wire machines or the squawk of the police radio. You could hear yourself think. Occasionally on slow news nights I would go back to our apartment for a bite to eat. My wife made clams casino one night and the filling in the clam shells was horrible. It wasn't her fault. The grocery store had mislabeled the freshness date. She asked "How does it taste?" After an attempt at diplomacy I said "It tastes like death on the half shell." Whereupon I grabbed a peanut butter and jelly sandwich and went back to work, happily with a title. I wrote this poem in 10 minutes on an old Olivetti typewriter. I was 25, writing police news and sports for the newspaper, in addition to obituaries. Writing obits is a standard formula story, but it can become tedious and depressing. So the subject matter of this poem, written on 12-10-83, has traceable antecedents.

ISOSCELES MAN

It's tough today to make the right decision.
Only in math can you reach geometric precision.
Often you're dangling at the end of a rope,
Feeling you lack patience, depth and scope.
But you fail to consider the considerable angles.
While the sword of Damocles sways and dangles.
Untrammeled, unhindered, a woebegone soul,
You consistently sacrifice the half for the whole.

The two equal sides of the isosceles man
Form a heart and a mind that strive for a plan.
Fate will construct a Euclidean space.,
You will find it if you're not caught in a race.
To the depths of your soul you must aim for the truth.
Use all that you know dating back to your youth.
Where will this leave you amid emotion and reason?
The vortex of time unfolds the passing seasons.

Isolation, desolation, consolation, youth.
Consummation, dedication, motivation, truth.
Deliberation, contemplation, rejuvenation, rage.
Manipulation, reciprocation, recrimination, cage.
You can rail against fate and wear the face of scorn.
Or you can get up and fight to find your unicorn.
It seems like Mercury's locked in retrograde.
While hope is alive your strength will not fade.

© 1983, 2011, Michael A. Incitti

NOTES: This poem was written on another slow news night a few weeks after "Death On The Half Shell," on 12-29-83, while outside a silent and heavy snow fell. The two works appear in the same entry because of their closeness in time, and similarity in theme. "Isosceles Man" is about being young and wondering what to do with the life God gave you. It encourages action while acknowledging we are all Isosceles Men and Women as we try to look into our own futures to chart our best course. But as Shakespeare's Hamlet tells Horatio, "There are more things in heaven and earth than are dreamt of in your philosophy."

CHAINED BY ALICE

She made monkey soup by the heat of a match.
It was cooked in a thimble – a very small batch.
We passed it between us and sipped it slow.
Before we knew it, the supply was low.

I said to Alice, our illustrious chef,
'The soup is gone, there's nothing left.'
She said 'Please go home, I have no more.'
'And when you leave please use the door.'

Bridge:

Her eyes told me it was time to leave.
She found her way, no need to grieve.
She wrapped her heart in aluminum foil.
I left through the window of our mortal coil.

Chorus:

Alice has a secret, one that she will never share.
Alice has a secret, you could ask her if you dare.
She knows I won't give her money anymore.
She knows I won't take where it's sunny like before.

Icarus flew too close to the sun.
Superman's work was never done.
Daedalus told his boy not to go.
Jor-El knew his son would make a good show.

Alice we are apes in ways untold.
Few of us relinquish the ways of the fold.
I'm always reminded of man's other half.
There's something sinister in Darwin's last laugh.

2ndBridge:

When I left today she threw away the chains.
All along the red brick streets it started to rain.
Night had fallen in every corner of the yard.
Not a soul was left for the changing of the guard.

Chorus:

Alice has a secret, one that she will never share.
Alice has a secret, you could ask her if you dare.
She knows I won't give her money anymore.
She knows I won't take her where it's sunny like before.

NOTES: I wrote the core of this work in 5 minutes on 5-21-85, 9:30 p.m., at the kitchen table of our apartment in Philadelphia, Pa. I was attending graduate school and teaching at Temple University. Some 27 years later I added both bridges, the first stanza to the second verse, and the chorus, all of which I wrote in 10 minutes on 9-11-12, at 6:30 a.m. in Mountaintop, Pa. This poem began with the title "Monkey Soup," which was really chicken soup with rice and carrots. But because the girl who cooked it, Alice, an anthropology major, had no recipe and assembled it from multiple sources, I jokingly referred to it as Monkey Soup. Alice, not her real name, had hosted a party at her home in a Philadelphia suburb. As she did not make enough soup, portions distributed were minuscule, hence the thimble reference. The tacit understanding then among her Bohemian guests was that we were chained by hunger and it would be survival of the fittest. Of Alice, our lovely hostess, it can be said that she tried.

PHOEBE'S SONG

Chorus:

Won't somebody save her from these chains of hate and tears?
Can't somebody help her to obliterate these fears?
Will someone please try to read between her lines?
Can someone pull her from despair to embrace the divine?

She doesn't want to do it,
But there's no other way.
Kids at school avoid her,
They don't know what to say.

Most teachers let it slide.
They pretend not to see her pain.
Principal says his hands are tied.
They have to catch them to arraign.

So what was she to do?
Put a sign on her back and wait?
There's no reasoning with laughing fools
When their minds are filled with hate.

She didn't know how it started.
She hadn't done anything wrong.
A boy liked her and she liked him,
Then these angry girls came along.

At first she tried to be nice to them,
Then she tried to forgive and ignore.
But their harassment progressed to constant duress —
Just existing became a monumental chore.

Chorus:

Won't somebody save her from these chairs of hate and tears?
Can't somebody help her to obliterate these fears?
Will somebody please try to read between her lines?
Can someone pull her from despair to embrace the divine?

She wished she could make a fresh start,
Go far away and never return.
But their daggers of hate kept ripping at her heart,
While few showed any concern.

It all began innocently,
A football star said he liked her.
A self-appointed jury found her unworthy,
And in their hatred they would concur.

Then came a day she dreaded.
They followed her as she walked home.
They threw things at her and they called her names,
And one of them hit her with a stone.

As she lay bleeding
They screamed her name and swore.
She tried to get up and run,
But they knocked her down some more.

She prayed for it to end,
And she wondered 'Why won't God listen?'
Those evil girls were snakes with rattles
Coiled and striking and hissing.

Chorus:

Won't somebody save her from these chains of hate and tears?
Can't somebody help her to obliterate these fears?
Will someone please try to read between her lines?
Can someone pull her from despair to embrace the divine?

Then it was dusk and quiet.
An icy wind began to groan.
Slowly she picked herself up,
Aching and afraid, she dragged herself home.

She climbed the stairs to her lonely room
With one thing only on her mind.
How would her loved ones feel when they find her?
How will they cope, those she leaves behind?

She was sorry, but she felt she didn't belong here,
Tossed like a doll in a storm of rage.
She'd cower through halls where smiles became sneers,
She had to free herself from that hateful cage.

Her future wasn't written, but she just wanted it to end.
She tried her best to overcome, when all she did was pretend.
She didn't want to do it, but to her there was no other way.
Some friends at school had tried, though no one knew what to say.

Saying goodbye wasn't really so hard –
Like an empty swing creaking in a cold and windy back yard.
Clouds of black pressed against an angry gray sky –
Couldn't she have chosen another day to die?

Chorus:

Won't somebody save her from these chains of hate and tears?
Can't somebody help her to obliterate these fears?
Won't somebody please try to read between her lines?
She was an open book at 15 and her cover never lied.
If she made it any clearer there'd be nothing left to malign.
Please take away her pain and let it be benign.
Won't somebody help her, where's her 'Catcher In The Rye?'
Can someone pull her from despair so she can embrace the divine?

NOTES: "Phoebe's Song" came to me on the evenings of 4-10 and 4-11, 2010. I originally wrote it in first-person from the perspective of a 15-year-old who took her own life because she was bullied by classmates. But I changed the voice to third-person objective because it seems more effective to have someone speaking on her behalf. Sadly, this lyrical poem was inspired by a true story that made national news. The topic of bullying has become all too prevalent in the nation's schools, as well as in other environments. I had followed the story and was very moved by it. Unlike Holden Caulfield's little sister Phoebe in J.D. Salinger's classic novel "The Catcher In The Rye," the girl in the story did not have a big brother, or a sister, who could take steps to insure her safety. No one heard her "song," her cries for help. It also put the spotlight on a Massachusetts school district that failed her completely. This child wanted to forgive and forget and move on. But her tormentors wouldn't let her. She never had a chance. I debated whether to include this work in the book because of its highly emotional and controversial nature. But the journalist in me said that's precisely why it should be here. I used New Journalism techniques to render the poem's literary elements within a unique structure. As with my anti-drug poem, "A Better Way," my target audience for "Phoebe's Song" is junior high and high school kids. The message is clear. All of life is precious. Stop the bullying!

STILL WATER

Intro.:

Along the horizon
City lights shine
Like stars on a clear spring night.
From high on a hill
Branches of trees
Sketch lines against the sky.
Her silhouette by a pool
Framed in the shadows of dusk,
She slips silently into the cool
Still water.

1st Verse:

Her eyes mesmerize,
Her seductive smile captures.
She strikes you like a wrecking ball,
Her face a slice of rapture.

Framed in style, tinted in grace,
But there are no dots to connect.
You meet her at a corner of your soul,
Where heart and mind redirect.

Stiletto heels in her purse,
A side she will not show.
She's aware she's not the first,
But her heart you'll never know.

Her eyes will make you wonder
And her carriage moves times three.
You're wired to her body,
She will never let you be.

You like the way she looks.
You like the way she feels.
You like the way she smells.
She's your air, your drink, your meal.

1st Bridge:

Harmless fantasy's
A one-sided deal.
By the end of the day
Her signals are sealed.
You run interference,
She plays parlor tricks.
She's been here before,
You are not in the mix.
It's not your turf.
She's on top of a wave
You're tossed in the surf.
It's not you she'll save.

Instrumental Bridge:

2nd Verse:

She took you by surprise
The day she walked out the door.
Said she had her reasons,
Maybe you've got yours.

Said she didn't have the words
To say the things she feels.
But living with you these past few years
Was something less than real.

You knew the time would come
And you won't stand in her way.
But you knew in your heart
It was just something to say.

You'd fall on her stilettos
And you'd chew her .32
For another night of rapture,
Another night by the pool.

2ⁿᵈ Bridge:

Carry that torch,
Hold that candle,
Burn it at both ends.
You're bound to get scorched,
Bound to lose the handle,
Easier to just be friends.
The one you want does not want you.
Come full circle, hold onto what's true.
You're always living in a parallel world.
You're trapped on the side that often loses.
Man in the moon says he don't really care,
Long as he gets what he chooses.

In love there's no sure bet.
It's always a tricky proposition.
One will fall, the other might catch.
Once set there's no juxtaposition.

No soul is really lost, you see.
Each in his time finds his way.
But how to arrive at finding that path
Is something no one can say.

NOTES: I had several ideas in my 'in progress' file and I awoke with a couple of stanzas in my mind on 5-6-13. The "…man in the moon…." stanza had come on 4-3-13 without a framework. The second bridge with the torch and the candle came on 5-7-13 while I was driving my car in the country after meeting with a client. By then the poem was almost complete. Once I could see what it was about it became a matter of editing and general literary masonry. The poem has an almost camera-eye feel to it in terms of content. Two 12-line bridges is unusual, , but there is no chorus to this poem. There is no concrete inspiration for this other than word play and a collection of impressions driving the theme.

PURGATORY

In dribs and drabs and fits and starts,
Boredom and curiosity nip at the heart.
Through eddies and currents and wrinkles in time,
She tried to find peace within a hollow pantomime.

She came here years ago from a life she could not bear
To a life she knew would never be what it seemed.
She never loved the man, but she tried hard to care.
So she settled into half of a dream.

The years went by and he up and died,
But she had checked out long before.
It wasn't long when another came calling.
He liked the house, so she opened the door.

They live on a road where homes are few,
But the houses are all the same.
It's a very neat and pleasant avenue.
Gnomes watch the gardens in the rain.

They rise before the morning dew,
Make coffee and listen for the trains.
From a broken porch swing they survey the view
Of the fallow fields that remain.

What might have been is too far away,
And what will be is better left unsaid.
There's nowhere to hide from what they see today.
They don't know that they've already made their bed.

Dreams of the innocent sit in corners by day.
Scattered visions and thoughts haunt her night.
She'd like to get away, but there's nowhere to go.
She'd like to say she tries to do what's right.

On the night they wed her husband couldn't sleep.
He went to the living room without a peep.
She found him on the couch asleep, TV on.
She lay in his arms until the stars were gone.

In dribs and drabs and fits and starts
Boredom and curiosity nip at the heart.
She'd like to find someone who could tell her story.
In the meantime she lives in a hollow purgatory.

NOTES: I wrote the stanza 'dribs and drabs' on the run on a Tuesday afternoon, 9-3-13. Then on 9-8-13 the above lines came to me and I connected them to the phrase 'dribs and drabs.' What results is a poignant look at a restless and enigmatic life that never really found its way. I wrote it in 30 minutes, from 1:30 to 2 p.m. at my office desk. The subjects for this work come from a variety of characters in literature, and with character as plot, they form their own brand of "Purgatory.

GONDOLA

I steer a boat all through the day.
My gondola's at the port of the canal.
I'm no stranger to love's many ways.
When Venus asks me I tell her I shall.

I navigate these waters
Through days of endless sun.
But even if it rains
My people still have fun.

I am not their salvation.
I am not their reprieve.
I am but a messenger
Who wears his heart on his sleeve.

My gondola waits at the water's edge
Beckoning all who come near.
Take a ride through these aquatic streets.
Relax and have no fear.

Through all of the years
And all of the fares,
Tears of joy have streamed
From love so rare.

Love asks for faith when stars are crossed,
Broken vows may never mend.
The poet said those who loved and lost
Have a spirit that always ascends.

Venus is more than a statuesque form;
She is the beauty that was ancient Rome.
Her eyes are discerning, but her heart is warm.
And she never wanders far from her home.

Her method is older than the ruins of time.
It's been here as long as man can remember.
When she's with you there are no mountains to climb,
And your fires burn bright without embers.

I do not question what she asks of me.
I am Charon, I am Cupid, I am Mercury.
I do the bidding of the goddess of love.
She gives me hope and gifts from above.

I steer a boat all through the day.
My gondola's at the port of the canal.
I am no stranger to love's many ways.
When Venus asks me I tell her I shall.

I navigate these waters
Through days of endless sun.
Venus blesses all the lovely young girls.
Someday she'll bring me one.

NOTES: "Gondola" was written over several days working late at night or early morning in mid-November. At first I wanted the protagonist to meet a woman and experience love and loss. But I realized that in keeping with Greek and Roman mythology and its ironies, his purpose should be to enable love to exist and to flourish, but not to experience it. The gondola was his instrument or gift, as is Pan's flute, Cupid's arrow, Mercury or Hermes' winged feet, or Charon's boat. So I edited out 16 lines that didn't fit and kept the focus on his role in service to Venus, the goddess of love. Her Greek name is Aphrodite. "Gondola" was an assignment I gave myself to discipline the creative process. I saw a news photo of a gondolier steering a gondola with the caption stating that it was one of the most romantic jobs in the world in one of the most romantic cities in the world, Venice. The gondolier had a man and a woman as passengers, and I thought it would be interesting to hear what he might have to say to them. Unlike "Objectified," which appears next and flowed line by line, "Gondola" had to be hammered out like a sculpture. Sixteenth century scholars asked Michelangelo, the great Italian painter, sculptor and driving force of the Renaissance, how he came to sculpt such incredible masterpieces like "The Angel," or the "Madonna." He said he thought about what he wanted to sculpt, and then he hammered away everything else.

OBJECTIFIED

1st Verse:

She walks the night in heels too high --
Her tightrope of social injustice.
She sees the light of lust in their eyes.
And she knows why they choose not to trust us.

The Eternal City hosts the oldest profession.
Some would call it a match made in heaven.
The clergy of Rome will hear your confession,
Then partake of wine and bread unleavened.

Chorus:

The hookers are objectified.
Their mini-skirts leave no doubt.
They do not seek to be sanctified.
They know what their lives are about.

Sexy and buxom or slender as cats,
They prowl the streets of the city.
From blue collar to diplomat,
Men are drawn in a way that's not pretty.

The call-girls sing their siren song.
The men find their alibis.
It can't be right, but it's never wrong.
These women are objectified.

2nd Verse:

It's a story told by clientele,
And it happens every minute.
Sometimes it can be hard to tell
If you're out or if you're in it.

Daughters of Mary Magdalene
With hearts that could repent.
In Vatican City their souls are clean.
They've earned their every red cent.

Chorus:

Bridge:

Angela didn't plan this life,
But it's always easy money.
She's got the look, she's got the knife,
When a guy wants more than honey.

Petite Sophia often wears a flower
As if she's going to a wedding.
Sometimes she charges by the hour,
And she always changes the bedding.

3rd Verse:

It's not the trade itself they hate
Because business must go on.
It's where it's done and who sees what
That has them up in arms.

The glory of Rome lies with its church --
Still the pillar of the modern world.
Who would think it would be left in the lurch
When a guy wants to get with a girl?

Chorus:

2nd Bridge:

A little bit of wind,
A little bit of rain,
A blessing for a song of hope
To take away the pain.

Anna Maria made the sauce,
She cooked what her husband liked.
Lena's guys all know who's boss
When she wears her leather and spikes.

Chorus:

The hookers are objectified.
Their mini-skirts leave no doubt.
They do not seek to be sanctified.
They know what their lives are about.

Sexy and buxom or slender as cats,
They prowl the streets of the city.
From blue collar to diplomat
Men are drawn in a way that's not pretty.

The call girls sing their siren song.
The men find their alibis.
It can't be right, but it's never wrong.
These women are objectified.

Epilogue:

She's a vignette of nocturnal scenes.
She's a ride in a red Lamborghini.
She plays roulette until it makes you scream.
You can't escape her even if you're Houdini.

NOTES: The idea for "Objectified" came from a news article about how prostitutes are proliferating throughout Rome causing embarrassment to the city's image as a seat of the Catholic religion. The article also covered sociological aspects of how women are treated within the framework of what is viewed as a criminal element. It proved an interesting topic for a song because of the ironies and the contrasts present. I wrote this work on 3-10-15 from 6 a.m. to 7:40 a.m. with minor revisions added at 10 a.m. From Fantine to Fanny Hill to Moll Flanders, literature is rife with characters who are prostitutes. I interviewed such a woman for "Harlot's Trilogy." When asked how I found my subject I quoted Woodward and Bernstein: "A good reporter never reveals his sources." "Objectified" is an exercise in divergent thinking, but some lines and stanzas have that ping. Because the poem is set in Italy I had to include a reference to that most objectified automotive work of art, the Lamborghini. This song came fluidly without getting stuck on structure, sound or meter. Like "Gondola," it came from news of the day in the Old World country that is Italy.

THE DENTIST

The dentist arrives early,
But he dreads the day ahead.
He's in his office at seven
He's in his prison by ten.

In between he sees the people
As they parade through his rooms.
His assistants do the work --
He would rather push a broom.

Sometimes he has some fun with them,
Moves patients like pieces of chess.
Manipulates and insinuates,
Then stops just short of duress.

The dentist leaves the office
At least an hour before noon.
It's not lunch that drives him out the door.
It's the thought of another tooth.

He sees them in his dreams at night.
The teeth won't let him sleep.
Molars and incisors chew on his mind.
Some days it makes him weep.

Once a year he recruits at a local school,
Scouts the finest then narrows it to one.
He invites her to his office and shows her his drill.
Who said dentistry wasn't fun?

His assistants are rather fetching.
He thinks he might have a go.
But the thought of a harassment suit
Is a feast for a wife who knows.

Another day, another dollar and there are lots of those.
Whirring machines hum and buzz – sometimes the drain overflows.
Soon the enamel nightmares are hanging everywhere.
He sees them in his wallet. He sees them in his hair.

One hygienist was getting a divorce.
She'd stay late with him to put away supplies.
There were allegations and innuendoes.
There were accusations and outright lies.

The dentist started to show signs of stress.
His hands were no longer steady.
Some older patients said he should take a rest.
He had to admit he was more than ready.

Today the dentist worked alone.
His hygienists didn't show.
Somehow he got through two patients,
And then a third he didn't know.

Just before lunch there was a fourth.
She rinsed then spit down the drain.
The dentist got up and excused himself,
Went to his office and blew out his brain.

NOTES: I wrote "The Dentist" in 30 minutes on 9-18-12, from 2 a.m. to 2:30 a.m. at my kitchen table. I hadn't had a dentist appointment, nor do I dislike dentists, most of whom I admire. The first four-line stanza came to me and wouldn't let me sleep. I decided I'd better get up and write those lines so I didn't forget them. Once the first 4 lines were set to paper, the rest of the poem flowed almost verbatim, 12 stanzas in all. There was no dentist in my mind as a model for the story. This narrative poem came solely from my imagination. The AABB rhyme scheme that appears in the 8th stanza differs from the established ABCB rhyme pattern to serve as foreshadowing that something has changed for the dentist, and that something is about to happen. This poem is one of my favorites.

SIDEBAR: In Northeast Pa. where we lived when I wrote this, there was a celebrated legal case 20 years earlier about a dentist who was tried for killing his wife after he had taken a mistress. This might have been in my subconscious as I wrote "The Dentist," but my ending echoes the likes of Edwin Arlington Robinson's masterpiece "Richard Cory," as opposed to the facts in the above case.

SIDEBAR: I've always had fairly good relationships with my dentists, with one exception. When I was a 9-year-old kid I was scheduled for a dental appointment, a routine cleaning. What was unusual was that the dentist I was scheduled to see was being investigated at the time for allegedly murdering his wife. Local police had no hard evidence, so everything that appeared in the papers was circumstantial. He was out on bail, but he kept his practice going to pay his legal fees. My friends in the neighborhood brought this to my attention. "It was in the paper, didn't you see it?" At the time I read only the sports section. "Hey, you wanna mess with this guy?" one of my friends said. "Why not eat an onion before showing up. He'll get done fast." It made sense to me, so I did just that, almost. Since eating a raw onion did not appeal to me, I made an onion sandwich slicing half an onion onto white bread with mustard on top. It wasn't half bad, and it had its intended effect. One of my buddies said, "I can smell your breath from 10 feet away. Damn, that's bad. You're good to go." We were quite a motley group. I'd like to say we were reminiscent of "Spanky and Our Gang" or the cartoon "Peanuts," but we did not have their gentle charm. We were edgy, and we did not take well to authority or convention. We were more like the kids in the cartoon "South Park." The four of us then trudged through the snow to the dentist's office. It was a winter's day and we had off from school for Christmas break. We showed up to an empty waiting room, boots covered with snow, and at least two of us were armed with icy snowballs. There was no secretary on duty. The dentist himself came out to the waiting room. "Which one of you is Michael?" I said "That's me." "Right this way," he said. I turned to one of my buddies and said "Oh shit." But I was done in 5 minutes. When I came back out my friends said "Told ya. Let's get outta here." We walked to the local candy store, Goody's, which was two blocks up the street from my Dad's barber shop. We had a Coke and pretzels and potato chips while we laughed about the snowballs that had melted all over the dentist's floor.

CHAPTER 9
A MINOR POET IN A MINOR KEY

WHY?

If God is love, then why can't we look upon his face?
If life is good, then why are there problems with race?
If dreams are sweet, then why do some live a nightmare?
If truth is near, then why are there so few who care?

If love is life, then why are so many alone?
If food is rife, then why is there hunger unknown?
If peace is key, then why are so many at war?
If law is just, then why are so many ignored?

If time heals all, then why are so many in peril?
If the good heed their call, then why are we haunted by terror?
If the world is rich, then why can't we cure disease?
If spirits are poor, why would we turn away with ease?

If it's time to reap, then why do so many still need?
If we sow what we keep, then why are there so many to feed?
If God is love, then why can't we look upon his face?
If hope is gone, then God has come into this place.
If all hope is gone, then God has come into this place.

© 2015, Michael A. Incitti

NOTES: I was in church listening to a sermon one Sunday and the preacher said that man cannot look upon the face of God else he might turn to stone. I got to thinking that if God loves us as his children wouldn't he want his children to look upon him while he bestowed good things to us or cared for us, like any parent would? In the Book of Genesis, Lot's wife is turned into a pillar of salt for looking upon what was perceived as evil against the warning of angels. So the line about not being able to look upon the face of God stuck with me. I'm not a theologian by any stretch, but I've always believed God was a benevolent being who may take many forms, but who always loves us, his children, unconditionally. And like any parent God probably likes it when we show love in return with a smile or a look of gratitude and happiness. I have to believe He, or She, will even entertain a question or two now and then, and prayers are always good. "Why?" was written on 8-5-15, 9-9:30 p.m., and 9-17-15, 11:45 to midnight.

SHAKE AWAY THE BLUES

She was always quite a looker
And he likes her a lot.
She's got a wicked tongue
That puts him on the spot.
She's got a way to knock him
Right out of his shoes.
But he can't shake away the blues.

She promises the world
Then she shows an empty hand.
All those images of love
Wash away like sand.
She's got lips of fire
And eyes you can't misconstrue.
That's why he can't shake away the blues.

Sometimes in the morning he awakes alone in bed.
The sun shines through the cracks in the blinds
And rays of light bounce off his head.
He searches his mind for a word or a phrase,
Something important he thought she said.
It trickles through his memory like water down a spout,
And pours itself on the pavement below
Where the light of day erases all doubt.
He still can't make sense of the conclusion he drew.
That's why he can't shake away the blues.

Yesterday he saw her walking,
Peering in shops along the street.
She seemed in quite a hurry,
And he wondered whom she might meet.
She's got legs he can't forget --
There's no other point of view.
No, he won't shake away the blues.

Tomorrow he will call her
When she takes her coffee break.
She really is quite lovely.
Her heart he won't forsake.
If she'd just pick up the phone
He could tell her all his news.
But he never will shake away the blues.

NOTES: "Shake Away The Blues" was written on an early morning in late spring in one draft with minimal editing. There was no subject or inspiration, just my imagination. I awoke with the words to the first 7 lines in my mind, and then visual images appeared for what was to follow and I just described what I saw in my mind's eye. The unique structure of 2 7-line stanzas, a 10-line bridge, then 2 more 7-line stanzas suits the subject well.

PATTY AND MARLENE

Intro.

Patty and Marlene, I loved you both
When we were kids of just thirteen.
The Lord took Patty when she was nineteen.
He took Marlene at age twenty-three.

1st Verse:

Patty would watch me play baseball
On a calm and peaceful summer's day.
After the game we'd walk and hold hands.
I never knew quite what to say.

She'd squeeze my hand and smile as we walked
Because talking didn't matter anyway.
Sometimes she'd speak of her piano,
And how she loved to play.

She'd learned a new song, John Lennon's "Imagine,"
And she played it just the other day.
She wore a white linen dress with tiny purple lilacs,
And her glasses on her nose in that funny sort of way.

Her voice soared through the auditorium.
It rang clear and bright and true.
Patty was perfect on every note and chord,
And she played the song all the way through.

Chorus:

If God is in his Heaven, He must have needed them there
To play for Him and to sing.
To be among the angels in harmony
Making music for the joy that it brings.

But I'll never understand why God took the girls
Before their lives were lived.
An alto on piano and a soprano on guitar,
Only this had they to give.

2nd Verse:

Marlene would watch me play basketball
On the courts of the junior high.
We were friends and I wanted us to be more,
But Marlene would never lie.

She loved Carole King's "Tapestry,"
And she played the songs as best she could.
Her parents bought her a six-string guitar,
A piece of heaven made of strings and wood.

Marlene took her guitar almost everywhere,
The gym, the classroom and the car.
If anyone was going to make it in music,
She was going to be our star.

One day in class she played "You've Got a Friend,"
And a winter beau helped her sing the song.
She played so well strumming chords like a bell,
The applause for her was loud and long.

Bridge:

I still see Marlene laughing.
I can still hear Patty sing.
Our lives went on while they became a memory
Of winters that ran into springs.
None of us knows God's decisions.
Fewer still have an inkling of His ways.
We can sit and wonder 'neath the sky that we are under,
Or we can honor and celebrate their days.

Chorus:

If God is in His Heaven, He must have needed them there
To play for Him and to sing.
To be among the angels in harmony
Making music for the joy that it brings.

But I'll never understand why God took them
Before their lives were lived.
An alto on piano, a soprano on guitar,
Only this had they to give.

3rd Verse:

Patty and Marlene, I loved you both,
Though we were kids of just thirteen.
The Lord took Patty when she was nineteen.
He took Marlene at age twenty-three.

The world is so very different now.
In many ways it stays the same.
Young boys will play, young girls will dream,
But today I put flowers on their graves.

© 2014, Michael A. Incitti

NOTES: With the exception of minor editing and recasting of one stanza, I wrote this entire poem in the car as my wife, Aprile, drove us home from a weekend in New England on June 28, 2014. I wrote "Patty and Marlene" that Sunday afternoon as we drove from Massachusetts to Connecticut to New York. I had a sense that something was working in my mind and would have to be written, so I asked my wife to drive. I had long wanted to write a poem for these two girls who have existed in my memory all these decades. This poem recounts events from 1972 and 1973 that live in my mind's eye as if they happened yesterday. It is the remembrance of a 13-year-old celebrating the innocence and splendor of childhood. It's interesting what a 13-year-old kid can perceive, but can't always express at the time. Both of these girls were good friends of mine, and I loved them as only a socially-awkward, athletic 13-year-old boy could. We were 8th and 9th grade classmates at Theodore Roosevelt Junior High School in Williamsport, Pa. That they are both forever etched in my memory is a testament to their enduring spirit, their unique and wondrous beauty, and their timeless humanity. We remained friends throughout high school, but fell out of touch when we all went to college. Upon returning home in the spring of 1978 I was devastated to learn that Patty had passed. Marlene passed a few years later, both far too young to go. What appears is almost verbatim from what I wrote in the first draft. Where the words came from, how these ideas coalesced on that day, I cannot say. But wherever the girls are, and I know they're in Heaven, I hope they like what I've written for them.

SOLILOQUY

I write at night while the world is silent.
And the moon is my only company.
I write at night in the deafening quiet,
And the music feeds my revelry.

Sometimes it comes like a soft spring rain,
This music that plays in my brain.
A one-man band in a corner of a room,
By this craft I am consumed.

I spend my nights trying to write a hit song.
By day I don't know if I'm right or I'm wrong.
The ideas are mine, I won't steal or rob.
I take care of business, and I keep my day job.

Contacts are few, year after year.
It leaves me writing songs that no one will hear.
There's no consolation, there's no adulation,
Just a lonely pursuit with a faint destination.

The record machine is distant and cold.
Capture the Zeitgeist before it gets old.
Or write something timeless, wistful and sweet
That sings in the ear and moves with a beat.

Then the turn of a phrase, a well-metered rhyme,
Accents and consonants move with rhythm in time.
It all starts again, these words in my head.
In my brain they ascend, and they drag me from my bed.

Like a fish on a line before you bring him ashore,
Words promise much, music asks for more.
Sometimes I wonder if it's all worth the fight --
Manuscripts and mayhem through a dark, sleepless night.

To write a song you must see, hear and feel.
Then thoughts submerge, like Hamlet's scene to steal.
Old Billy Shakespeare never had it this tough.
He could write what he wanted, and he never said enough.

I don't know where all this will lead.
But when it calls day or night I must proceed.
Only time will tell if my heart is right
To lead me from the darkness into this light.

Sometimes there's solace in the world mundane.
Sometimes answers lie on a simpler plane.
Wish I knew what makes me write this stuff.
Seems the earthly world is never enough.

Have I fooled myself with flights of somnambulant transcendence?
Or does my work have merit, so I really shouldn't end this?
These are questions to ask of a philosophical soul.
But the answers lie far beyond my mortal control.

When you ride that train to the edge of your soul
You arrive at a place that few ever know.
Your task is to write and record what you see.
It comes in a flash, and it never comes free.

Every day is someday when you're driven by a dream.
It can come within your reach if you find the right team.
Subjective introspection can pay big dividends.
It arrives in a moment, sometimes with a friend.

Carole King and I will collaborate.
I'll hang with Smokey and his clown.
Stevie Wonder and I will have notes to compare.
Billy Joel will marvel at what he found.

Rhymin' Simon will give me a call.
Paul Williams will shoot the breeze.
Jimmy Webb will say we must get together.
Paul McCartney sends regards from the queen.

All these things just might take place
If the songs I write will sell.
In the meantime I'll return to my room
And in my keyboard corner dwell.

I rarely wear a tie.
My world is never on a string.
But I'm the bishop of possibility.
My message will make you sing.

No sleight of hand,
No whistle in the dark.
A consciousness to expand
Is not a walk in the park.

Be careful what you wish for.
The price may be high.
I've walked a lonely corridor
Toward a truth you can't deny.

Take me far away.
The world I will explore.
I will free your dreams.
I will help your spirit soar.

For I am the bishop of possibility.
I'm the architect of extremes.
I'm the contract killer of a narrow mind.
I'm the bridge from your soul to your dreams.

I write at night while the world is silent.
And the moon is my company.
I write at night in the deafening quiet,
And the music feeds my revelry.

NOTES: Initially I did not include "Soliloquy" in this book. But I liked it. Despite its relative length it builds to a type of crescendo at the end amid evocative and sometimes powerful lines and phrases. I wrote most of this poem on Nov. 24 and 25, 2012. Editing was done on Dec. 8, 9, and 10, and on Jan. 27, 2013. This lyric poem came about in response to a request from a songwriting friend who said "Why not write a song or a poem about the process of songwriting?" So I did.

I SEE YOU

I see you in me.
Do you see me in you?
Spaghetti O's on your nose,
A red wagon built for two.

A shovel in the spring
To plant trees and flowers.
Grandpa Jay's Army jeep
To ride and ride for hours.

A bat and a glove
And a game of catch.
A ball to throw
And a hat to match.

Driveway basketball
And summers at the shore.
Was enough for me,
But you always wanted more.

I see you in me.
Do you see me in you?
Spaghetti O's on your nose,
A red wagon built for two.

A black tux and cologne for the prom,
A wrist corsage for her.
Suddenly a man, you even had a tan,
I would have been proud to be your chauffeur.

Then you went away
To a school where night was day.
And in many ways
You never returned.

We were waiting as an act of will.
The time was late, there was a chill.
But we would not quit at all until,
Your umbrage adjourned.

I see you in me.
Do you see me in you?
Spaghetti O's on your nose,
A red wagon built for two.

A child was born in Bethlehem
More than two-thousand years ago.
Our son came home on a Christmas Day.
Never again will his spirit roam.

I see you in me.
Do you see me in you?
Spaghetti O's on your nose,
And a red wagon built for two.

NOTES: I wrote this poem on 11-11-15 and 12-31-15 for my son, Marc.

As much as he liked getting a ride in a wagon or a wheelbarrow, my son, Marc, also liked to pull his own wagon. Today he pulls his own weight, and then some, with his work in medicine and health care. With our son we are blessed.

THE APPLE CART

He keeps a tooth
In a soap dish by the toothpaste.
With regularity in bed by eleven,
Separate beds, yet pushed together.

She watches the late show
In a tattered pink robe, black ankle socks,
And dog-chewed slippers, and retires
After Nelson Eddy and Jeanette McDonald have
Sung their last song.

He listens all day
While meliorating the heads of his friends.
Locks the shop door, gets milk and bread,
Then heads home with news of his friends.

She types, computes, audits and mails.
Records debits and credits and payrolls --
The boss won't buy donuts
And the receptionist is pregnant.

He putters with wood in the cellar after dinner.
She watches Jokers Wild and roots for the winner.
The son came home from college today
And upset the apple cart in his usual way.
How many apples fell this time?
How many more till it's really a crime?
And is the cart filled with apples indeed?
Or are they cores from the past, still holding seeds?

NOTES: I wrote "The Apple Cart" in March 1979 when I came home for spring break. It just came to me and I wrote it in a burst in 25 minutes, then I took 10 minutes to edit it and it was done. It arose from a disagreement. My Mom and Dad kept small steaks in a freezer downstairs. For some reason I would eat sparingly during the day – 7Up, cheese, crackers, an apple -- but by late afternoon I was ravenous. So I would cook a small steak, smother it in ketchup and Worcestershire sauce and have at it with a side of Italian bread and butter. This did not sit well with Mom and Dad. "He's eating steak as a snack. Those are for MEALS!" Well, after eating and then having a new one torn for me, I went to my room and wrote the above. For a 20-year-old kid and an early effort, it's not too bad. My Mom liked it a lot. She had a friend of hers copy it in some sort of calligraphy with oak leaves and designs around it. It was supposed to look like an apple tree, but I couldn't figure out what it was. Then she had it framed and she hung it on the wall in my bedroom in the space formerly occupied by a nice picture I had of a chimpanzee in a lab coat holding test tubes. Frankly, I preferred the picture of the monkey. "The Apple Cart" appears with the poems "Sunday Best," "The Barber," "Sunday Lunch," "Summer Brunette," and "1025,"all as tributes to my Mom and Dad.

BOHEMIANS AND ANARCHISTS

Bohemians are often
An interesting lot.
They don't sit around and think
About what they ain't got.
Sometimes they can solve
The problems of the globe.
And they do it without
Any ring on their lobes.
A gallon of wine and
A night playing cards
Brings answers unheard
From the avant-garde.

Anarchists by contrast
Are loud and annoying.
Their words are direct,
Never clever and cloying.
They shout and they smolder,
They rave and they bluster.
By morning their ideas
Have lost all their luster.
In the end they slink away
Hurt and dejected.
As if their very core
Had been strongly rejected.

I'm a bohemian,
Whatever that means.
Transcendental, continental
Flights fueled by caffeine.
Sometimes imagination
Makes it hard to see reality.
I write it all down as fast as I can,
Before it gets lost in carnality.
Sleep is a precious commodity.
When I was young they said I didn't need it.
Talent may reflect profundity,
But one must continually feed it.

Epilogue:

Now I lay me down to sleep.
I pray the Lord my soul to keep.
If I should rise before I wake,
I want you to know I ate all the cake.

NOTES: I wrote "Bohemians and Anarchists" on 11-9-15, from 10 to 10:25 p.m. I was thinking about my old friends from college days and it occurred to me that we were all Bohemians who showed a particular disdain for anarchists, of which there were many at the time.

I NEED YOU

I need you,
You've heard these words before.
I need you,
Each day I say it more.
Just don't forget,
Your love is with me yet.
I'm always there, I'll always care, without regret,
I need you.

Chorus:

One-hundred forty-five miles away,
One-hundred forty-five miles to say,
Need you by my side,
Gonna put away my pride,
Gonna give you everything,
You are my song to sing.

2nd Verse:

I need you,
We're talking on the phone.
I need you,
Still another night alone.
You have no need to fear.
Even though your voice is clear
Soon I'll hold you near,
I need you.

Chorus:

One-hundred forty-five miles away,
One-hundred forty-five miles to say,
Need you by my side,
Gonna put away my pride,
Gonna give you everything,
You are flowers in the spring.

Bridge:

We took our time,
Went turtle slow.
Our laughter rhymes,
And you should know.
Love like ours happens
Once in a light year.
To Jupiter and back
We'll find a new frontier.
I need you.

3rd Verse:

I need you,
To love me the way you do.
I need you,
Like birds need trees and skies need blue.
Darling we were meant to be.
When you smile it's clear to see,
There is no I, there's only we,
I need you.

Chorus:

NOTES: While reviewing notes for the present manuscript I found this song on staff paper with musical accompaniment. The music was bad. Apparently I wrote it long before I learned how to play the piano. Still, the words were fair for an early effort by a 21-year-old kid. I wrote this song in April 1980. I edited, recast and restructured "I Need You" from 8 to 9 p.m. on 11-16-15 for inclusion in this book. Originally I wrote it as a gift to my future wife, Aprile, when I visited her at her home, which was 145 miles away from the college we attended. She was pleasantly surprised when I gave it to her in an envelope, written on a legal pad in longhand. In my best Stan Laurel voice I said "Well, you've stolen my heart." Then she read it. My most candid and unsparing critic, she smiled a Mona Lisa smile, and said she liked it.

AWAKENING

In the attic of his mind lay a narrow corridor --
A limousine of endless possibility.
Between the pull of the moon and the weight of the earth,
He felt a calm yet distant symmetry.

He did not fear the darkness of his room.
For it was the same as what was there in the light.
The early spring moon drove the boy from his bed,
And he bathed in the silent orb's sight.

Ten-thousand suns would rise and set.
Ten-thousand twilights would fly.
On a day with a ball and a backyard slope of grass,
He would sit and watch the clouds go by.

Ten-thousand more suns would rise and set.
Ten-thousand more nights would fall.
The odyssey of his imagination
Would finally reach its port of call.

NOTES: I wrote this poem on Dec. 30, 2015, from 2:50 p.m. to 3 p.m. after I drove a package to the post office. I saw a 30-foot black stretch limo coming the other way and these lines came to me immediately.

1025

At 1025 I always felt alive.
I'd rise facing the sun from the east.
With the woods to my left and my cousins to the right
It was sometimes as quiet as a priest.

From our little split level
At the top of a hill,
I'd ride a bike or a skateboard,
Until I took a spill.

At the base of the incline
Was a four-way intersect.
With friends at every corner
There was always a game to dissect.

At the four-way stop
Was a street-lamp bright.
We'd play foursquare or kick-the-can
Deep into a tree-lined summer night.

Neighborhood picnics in the 1960s were
Across the street in a vacant wooded lot.
Bonfires, touch football and baseball
Competed with the luck of the pot.

Summers were spent playing cards or Monopoly
On front porches of brick and wood.
But it was baseball or basketball at the school yard,
Where your presence was understood.

To the east was Andrew Jackson Elementary.
To the west, Theodore Roosevelt Junior High.
A kid could walk or ride a bike where he wanted to go.
It was a time and a place that today's money can't buy.

At 1025 my dreams were alive.
I'd sing with my record albums and my 45s.
They'd laugh at me from the sidewalk below.
But they had to admit it was a pretty good show.

I never thought much about going away.
But I knew the time would come someday.
I can still hear my father at dusk on a summer night
Calling for me to come home, and I knew he was right.

NOTES: As 1025 was the house number of my childhood home, this poem is another tribute to both my Mom and my Dad. But since I wrote it on Veteran's Day, 11-11, this work appears mainly in honor of my Dad.

A MINOR POET IN A MINOR KEY

A minor poet in a minor key,
Speaks of one who has humility.
It says that time is of the essence.
It seeks to capture incandescence.

All of life is a poet's canvas.
The tiniest spider in the smallest crevice,
Can become a source of meter and rhyme,
And can fix a word picture in a reader's mind.

The search for truth and stories to tell,
Becomes a part of you like a Hermit crab's shell.
A brief conversation is an ode to a pitcher.
One is never in it to become any richer.

A chance meeting becomes a wistful love song.
Something so right can never be wrong.
Then two women in a grocery line
Tell a story of lust and of days gone by.

A lover of words and of lexicon sweet,
Gives voice to the beauty that the world bequeaths.
Echoes of music and rhythms ring
As constant reminders of songs to sing.

A story recounted by one who was loved
Becomes a tribute in honor of those now above.
This quest never ends, you must understand.
A story in the news can drive pen to hand.

A dog or a cat or a trusted friend
Can inspire this tired back to bend
To the task of answering the call of verse.
It comes at all hours sometimes like a curse.

But it must be done like keeping a child fed.
To not respond would deny him milk and bread.
Tender memories of girlfriends past
Become the words of a phrase that lasts.

Some may think that to accept this call
Is to forego life and to put up a wall.
But the opposite's true, in life I'm immersed.
The tiniest atom can be turned into verse.

The act of creation is its own reward,
Like the fleeting sadness of a minor chord.
It comes in a flash like a spark in the night.
The couplets align as my spirit takes flight.

It takes me to places I may never go.
Imagination suffices in lieu of the show.
With all these ideas swimming round in my head,
It's a wonder I remember what anyone said.

So a minor poet in a minor key
Is really a beautiful thing to be.
It's a gift from God that I must obey.
The minor poet is me, forever and a day.

NOTES: "A Minor Poet In A Minor Key" is the title of the book, and of this poem that encapsulates and echoes some of the parts that comprise the whole. Of my book it must be said there was some assembly required as I organized my poems thematically into evenly divided chapters. The effect was greater form with a more cohesive and accessible structure overall. The poem "A Minor Poet In A Minor Key" came to me on the morning of Nov. 3, 2015, from 8 to 9 a.m., as it happens, a very good time to write.

Usually I write longhand on a legal pad when an idea comes to me. The next step in refining the work is to type it out on the computer, or on a 1939 Royal typewriter given to me by my Mom – the same one she used when she was a secretary. I learned how to type on this wonderful little 20-lb. piece of cast iron and steel. Thanks Mom. The minor poet is me.

AFTERWORD

A discerning reader might note that among all 101 lyric poems through 99 entries in this manuscript, none of the copyrights for my creative work occur within the decade of the 1990s. I did, however, copyright my dissertation in 1991, an onerous tome of approximately 450 academic pages that rests comfortably in the library at Temple University in Philadelphia. But I'm still a loyal Owl. There are two reasons for my lack of creative work in the '90s. I was working in finance during a highly volatile era of the stock market, and I was active with my children and in the community coaching baseball and basketball. My copyrights span 1978-1985, and 2006-2016. In between, my wife and I had kids. More often than not, I would work two jobs as primary and secondary sources of income, as in teaching part-time at a college while working in finance. My work and volunteer coaching absorbed all of my thoughts, time, energy and abilities such that little was left for creative pursuits. It was not until I secured the financial licenses that enabled me to run my own business and to devise my own work environment that I became free to return to my creative roots. I was overjoyed to discover that my creativity never really left me. It had just gone on hiatus for a while. So I went back to work on my craft, bringing with me a deeper perspective and a higher level of discipline.

The source of where many of the poems on these pages came from is still a mystery to me, even after 42 years of working with the art of poetry. Like time itself, music and poetry have been good friends who have walked with me through the decades. It's as if I have lived in two dimensions simultaneously – the physical world, and the transcendent, metaphysical world inhabited by music and literature. For me, there's no need to reconcile this duality. It exists, and I embrace it.

Just as my good friend and fellow Temple Owl, Greg Rai, from Long Island, N.Y., takes a band out with an electrifying guitar riff, his words will take us out.

"I have known the author of this work for 38 of my 57 years. I can assure you that this volume represents only a small portion of that which works in his fertile imagination. I am happy to see that Mike's poetry did not remain a remnant of his youth, but is often a portal to his youth and to all those time passages throughout his rich and varied life.

"A Minor Poet In A Minor Key" is highly readable, entertaining, sometimes humorous, and filled with some of most well-crafted poetry and lyrics that I've ever read. Coupled with unique stories about their creation, there is an artistic benevolence and an intrinsic sense of joy on every page.

"Perhaps our humanity comes with a responsibility to attempt to express its meaning in ways that go beyond the mundane and the temporal. Whatever the reason, I am pleased that my friend did not neglect the tug of that drive to create and to compose his work. I am delighted that he did not overlook what was in his heart and in his mind that needed to be expressed. I am grateful that he believed. I feel blessed and honored to be able to witness that one of us has succeeded in expressing those moments of his life in which he was a tributary to the ocean of the eternal.

"I thank him for his words, and for his friendship."

March 2016

AUTHOR BIO

Michael A. Incitti holds an undergraduate degree from Bloomsburg University of Pa. in English, American literature, with a minor in journalism. After working on Pennsylvania newspapers for 5 years as an award-winning reporter and sportswriter, he undertook graduate study at Temple University in Philadelphia. He completed a master of journalism degree, and a doctoral degree in mass communications and media law, both of which were earned on teaching and research scholarships. As a college professor for 15 years, he conducted award-winning research, and he was a well-regarded and innovative instructor. For the last 21 years he has worked in finance as an investment adviser and owner of his own firm. But of all that he has done, he is most proud of the sum and substance of his creative work, the poetry collection presented in this volume. Michael is the father of three children, a son and twin daughters, with his wife, Aprile. They make their home in Rehoboth Beach, Delaware.

www.ingramcontent.com/pod-product-compliance
Lightning Source LLC
La Vergne TN
LVHW091249080426
835510LV00007B/176